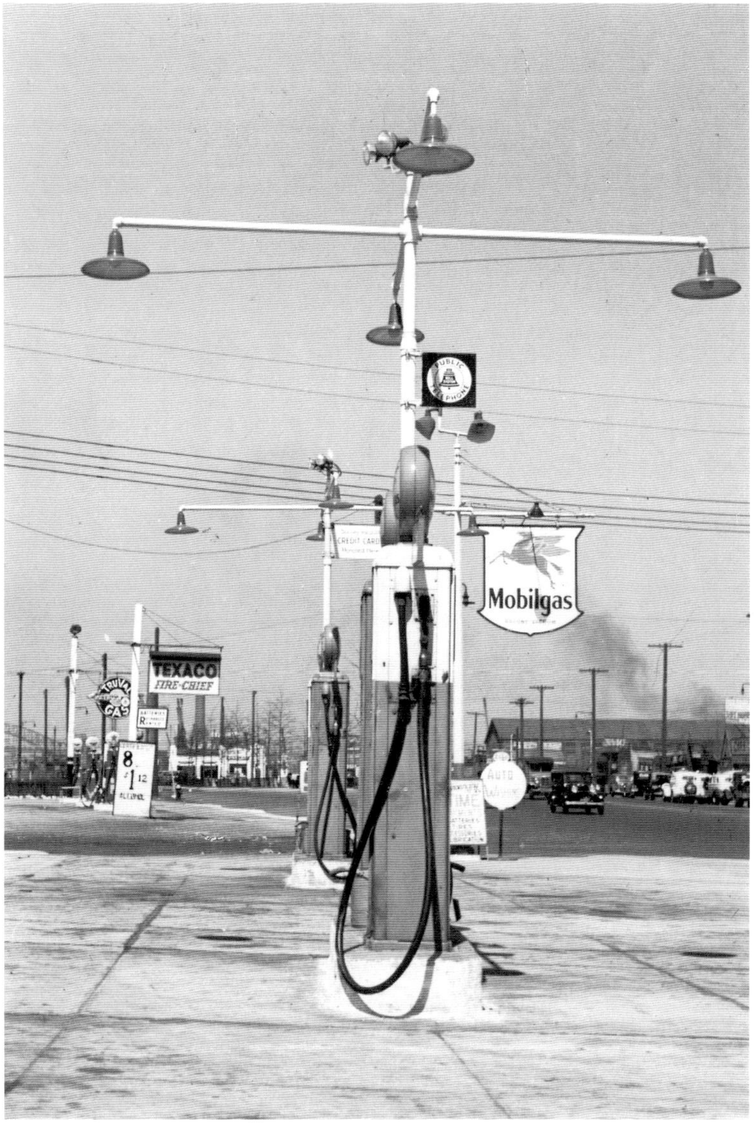
TEXACO
FIRE-CHIEF
Mobilgas

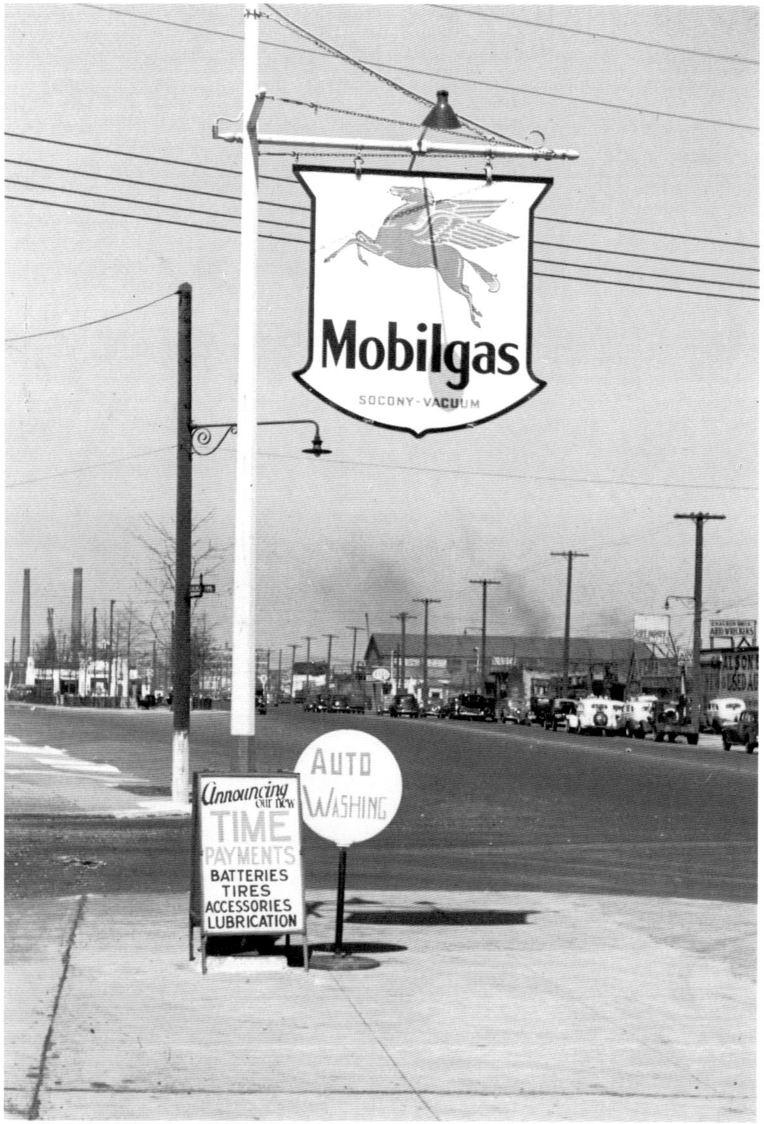
Mobilgas
SOCONY-VACUUM
Announcing our new
TIME
PAYMENTS
BATTERIES
TIRES
ACCESSORIES
LUBRICATION
AUTO
WASHING

AN AFTERNOON IN ASTORIA

BY RUDOLPH BURCKHARDT

The Museum of Modern Art, New York
Distributed by D.A.P./Distributed Art Publishers, New York

THIS BOOK IS PUBLISHED ON THE OCCASION OF THE OPENING OF MOMA QNS,
THE MUSEUM OF MODERN ART'S FACILITY IN QUEENS, NEW YORK

The publication is supported by a generous grant from Adam Bartos

Produced by the Department of Publications, The Museum of Modern Art, New York
Edited by David Frankel
Designed by Hsien-Yin Ingrid Chou
Production by Chris Zichello
Direct digital-capture scans by Kelly Benjamin, Kimberly Marshall Pancoast, and John Wronn
Printed and bound by Trifolio S.R.L., Verona
Type set in FB Interstate
Printed on 170 gsm Xenon Scheufelen

Library of Congress Control Number: 2002103314
ISBN: 0-87070-436-2

Published by The Museum of Modern Art
11 West 53 Street, New York, New York 10019

Distributed in the United States and Canada by D.A.P./Distributed Art Publishers, New York
Distributed outside the United States and Canada by Thames & Hudson Ltd, London

Cover: Rudy Burckhardt. Untitled. From *An Afternoon in Astoria*. 1940
Frontispiece: Rudy Burckhardt. Untitled. From *An Afternoon in Astoria*. 1940

Printed in Italy

FOREWORD

Glenn D. Lowry
Director, The Museum of Modern Art

In June 2002, The Museum of Modern Art opens MoMA QNS, a state-of-the-art facility for the care, study, and display of the Museum's great collection. This and the P.S. 1 Contemporary Art Center, our affiliate, give us an important presence in Queens. To celebrate the event, the Museum has reached out to many organizations and communities in the borough–and of course to artists, who have been invited to create a variety of interventions related to the new facility.

Rudy Burckhardt (1914-99) needed no invitation to discover Queens. Not long after he arrived in New York from his native Switzerland in 1935, he found his way across the East River to a place that perfectly suited the quiet, affectionate sensibility of his early experimental films and photographs. Among the gems of Burckhardt's work in Queens is his exquisite album *An Afternoon in Astoria*, of 1940. We have been eager to publish the album ever since purchasing it from the artist, in 1993, after the Museum's retrospective of Burckhardt's films in 1987. The opening of MoMA QNS provides the ideal occasion for this publication, which is designed in the same format and roughly the same size as the original spiral-bound album.

Three people have played instrumental roles in realizing this project, and I thank them enthusiastically: Yvonne Jacquette, Rudy Burckhardt's widow and thoughtful guardian of his artistic legacy; Adam Bartos, whose generous contribution has made the publication possible; and Mary Lea Bandy, the Museum's Deputy Director for Curatorial Affairs, who has done a masterful job of nurturing artists' interventions at MoMA QNS.

I am particularly grateful to Sarah Hermanson Meister, Associate Curator, Research and Collections, in the Department of Photography for the painstaking care with which she has carried out the project, and for her thoughtful commentary on the album and its place in Burckhardt's work.

ACKNOWLEDGMENTS

Sarah Hermanson Meister

To learn and write about Rudy Burckhardt has been an exceptional experience. Burckhardt engendered such admiration and warm feelings among all who had the pleasure of knowing him that every person I contacted seemed genuinely delighted to talk with me–if only for the opportunity to remember their relationship with him. Of the many people I spoke with I am particularly indebted to five. Christopher Sweet facilitated the Museum's purchase of Burckhardt's photographs–including *An Afternoon in Astoria*–in 1993. Ron Padgett was generous with his time and insight, providing me with copies of his own research and (as yet unpublished) writing on Burckhardt. Edith Schloss kindly allowed me to read her recollections of Burckhardt, his albums, and his collaborations with Joseph Cornell. Robert Storr, Senior Curator in the Museum's Department of Painting and Sculpture, provided candid and eloquent commentary on Burckhardt and his work. Yvonne Jacquette's unfailing support of this project deserves special note, from her willingness to open the archives of Burckhardt's estate to her warm and helpful responses to my many questions.

I am sincerely appreciative of the contributions of several people within the Museum without whom this project would not have been possible. David Frankel's thoughtful editing, Chris Zichello's sensitive and sensible production, and Hsien-Yin Ingrid Chou's perfectly pitched design have all combined to highlight the understated beauty of Burckhardt's work. I thank Harper Montgomery for her friendship and counsel, Kristine Haugaard Nielsen for her indispensable and imaginative research, and Charles Silver for arranging numerous screenings of Burckhardt's films. Amy McLaughlin's energy and organizational skills have been crucial throughout the project. Deputy Director for Curatorial Affairs Mary Lea Bandy supplied immediate and unwavering enthusiasm for Burckhardt's accomplishments in photography and film, making no obstacle insurmountable. The support and input of Peter Galassi, Chief Curator in the Department of Photography, were invaluable.

AN AFTERNOON IN ASTORIA

BY RUDOLPH BURCKHARDT

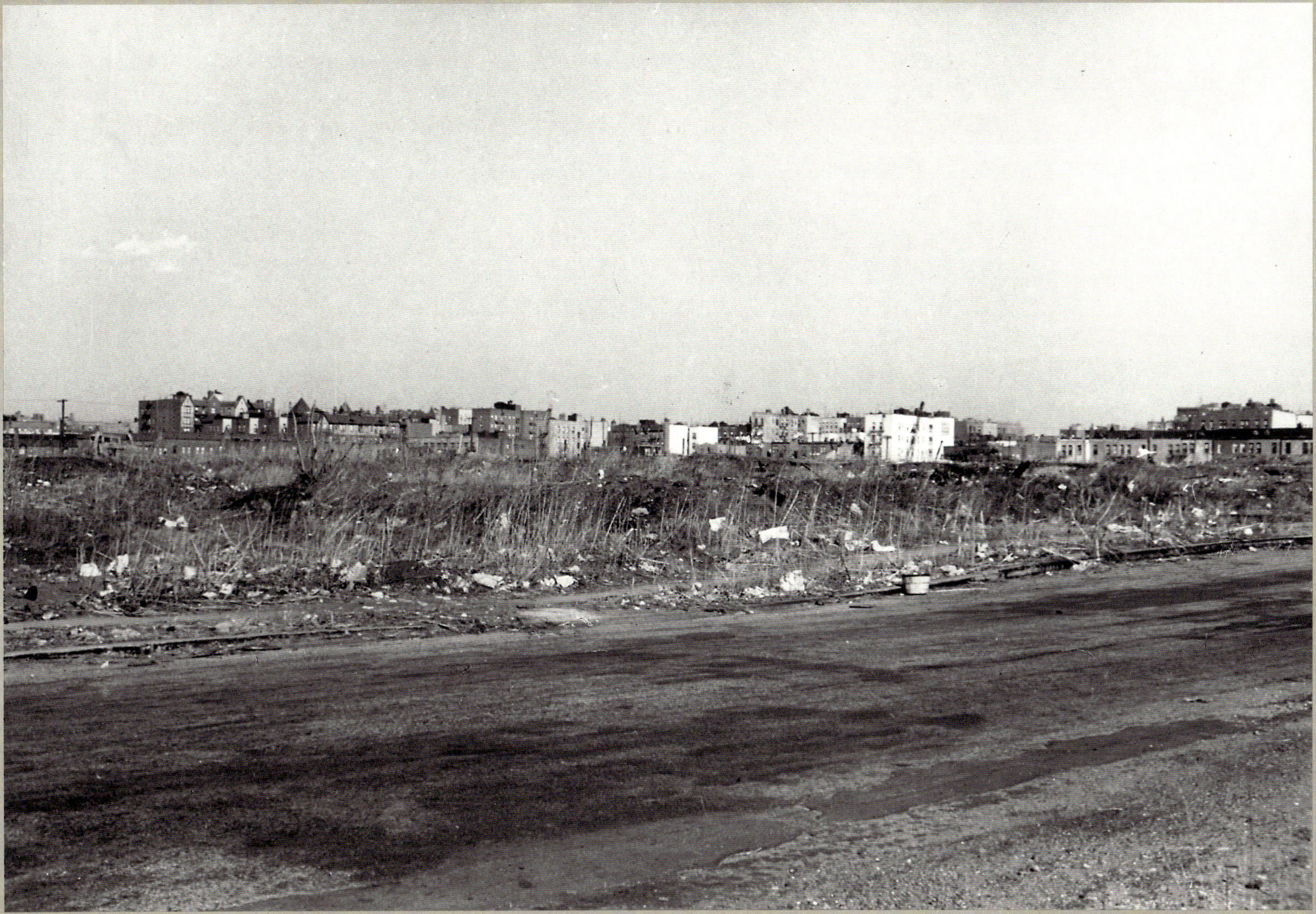

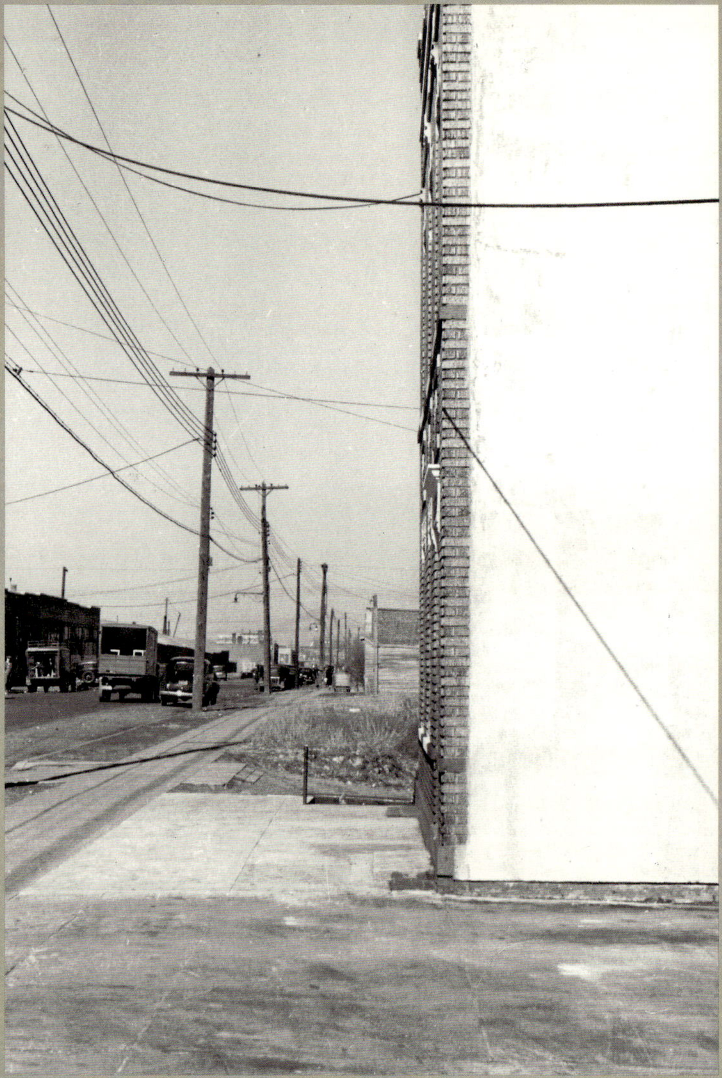

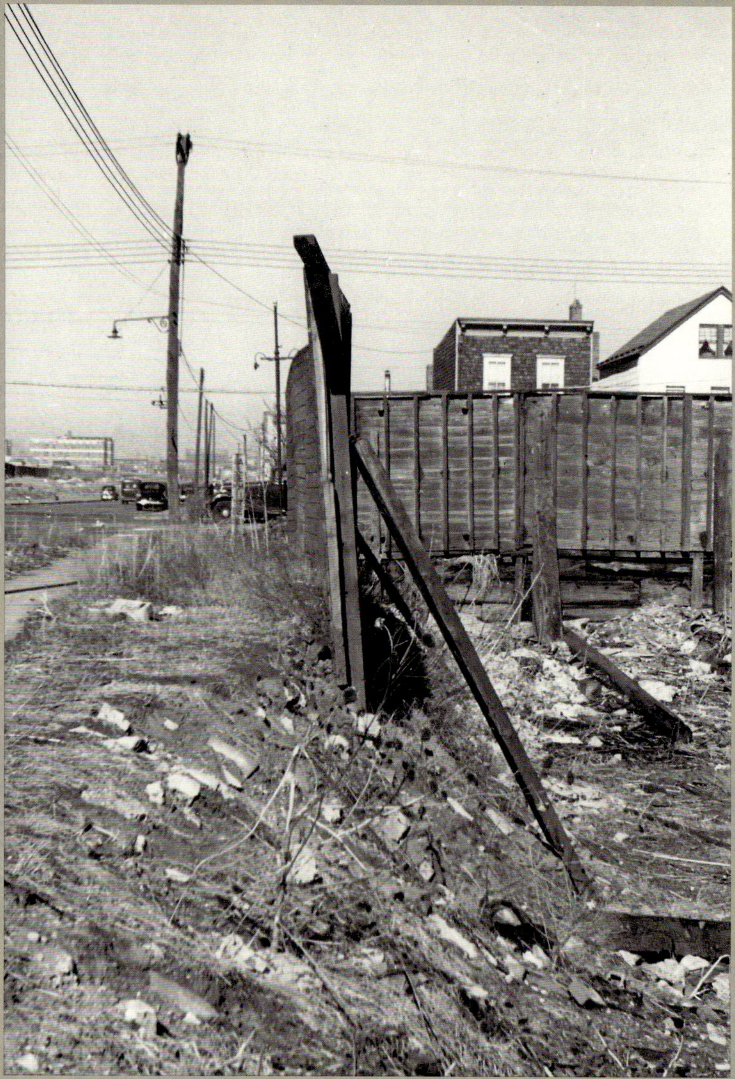

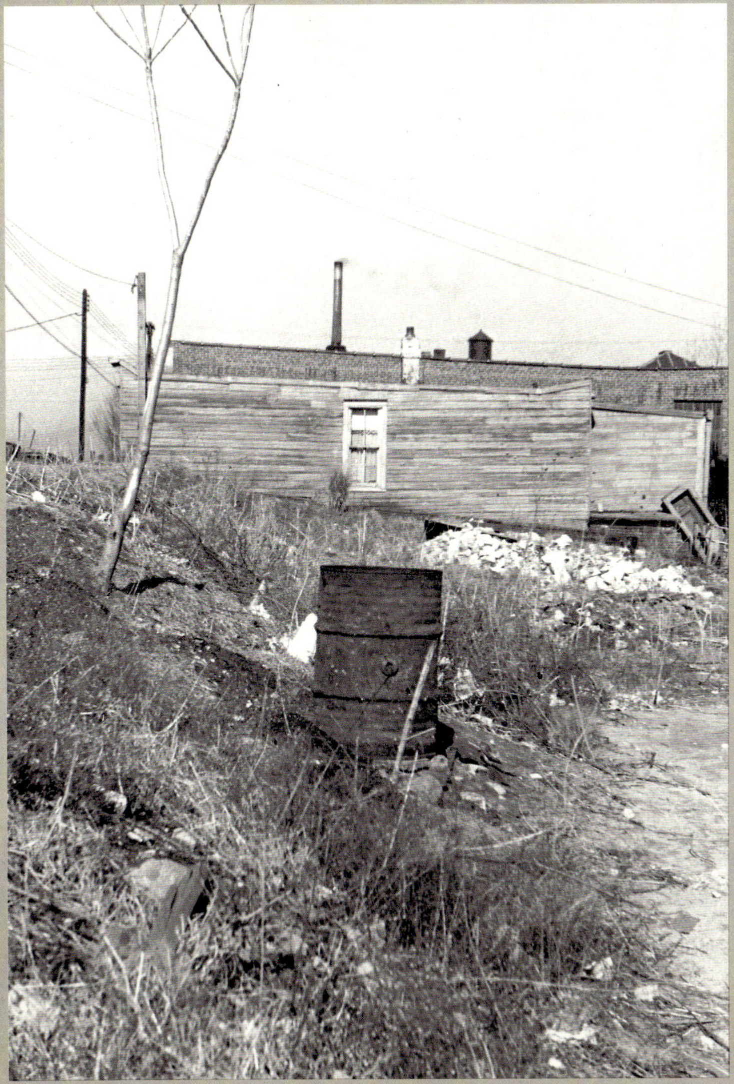

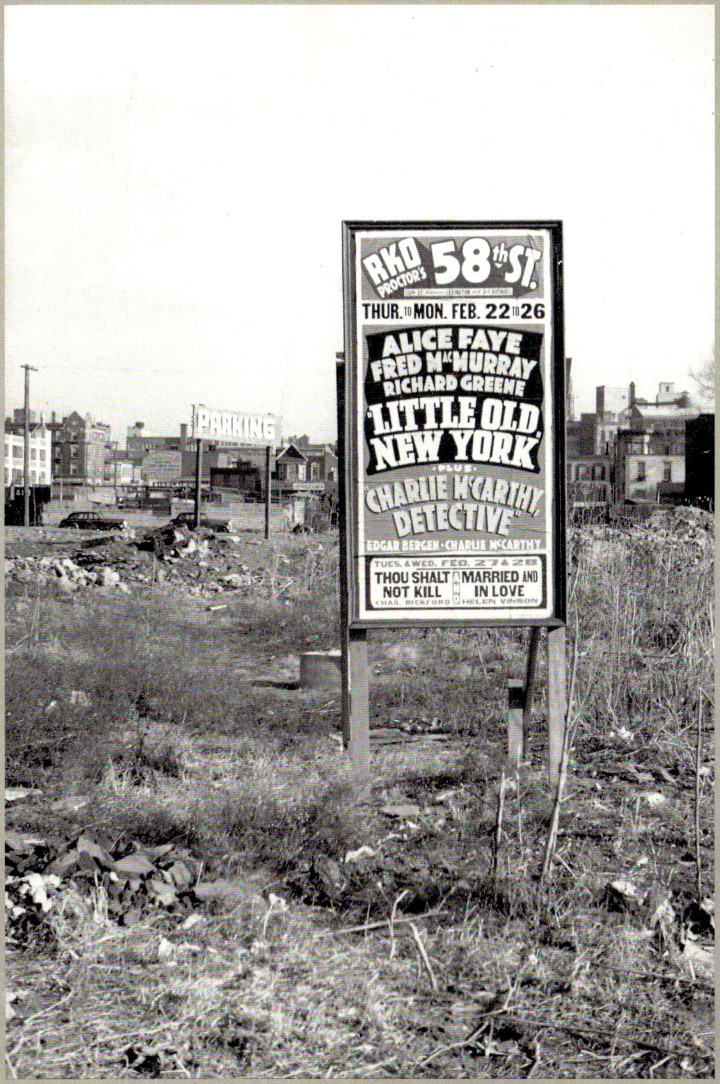
PARKING
RKO PROCTOR'S 58th ST.
THUR. TO MON. FEB. 22 TO 26
ALICE FAYE
FRED MacMURRAY
RICHARD GREENE
"LITTLE OLD NEW YORK"
PLUS
"CHARLIE McCARTHY, DETECTIVE"
EDGAR BERGEN · CHARLIE McCARTHY
TUES. & WED. FEB. 27 & 28
THOU SHALT NOT KILL
CHAS. BICKFORD
AND
MARRIED AND IN LOVE
HELEN VINSON

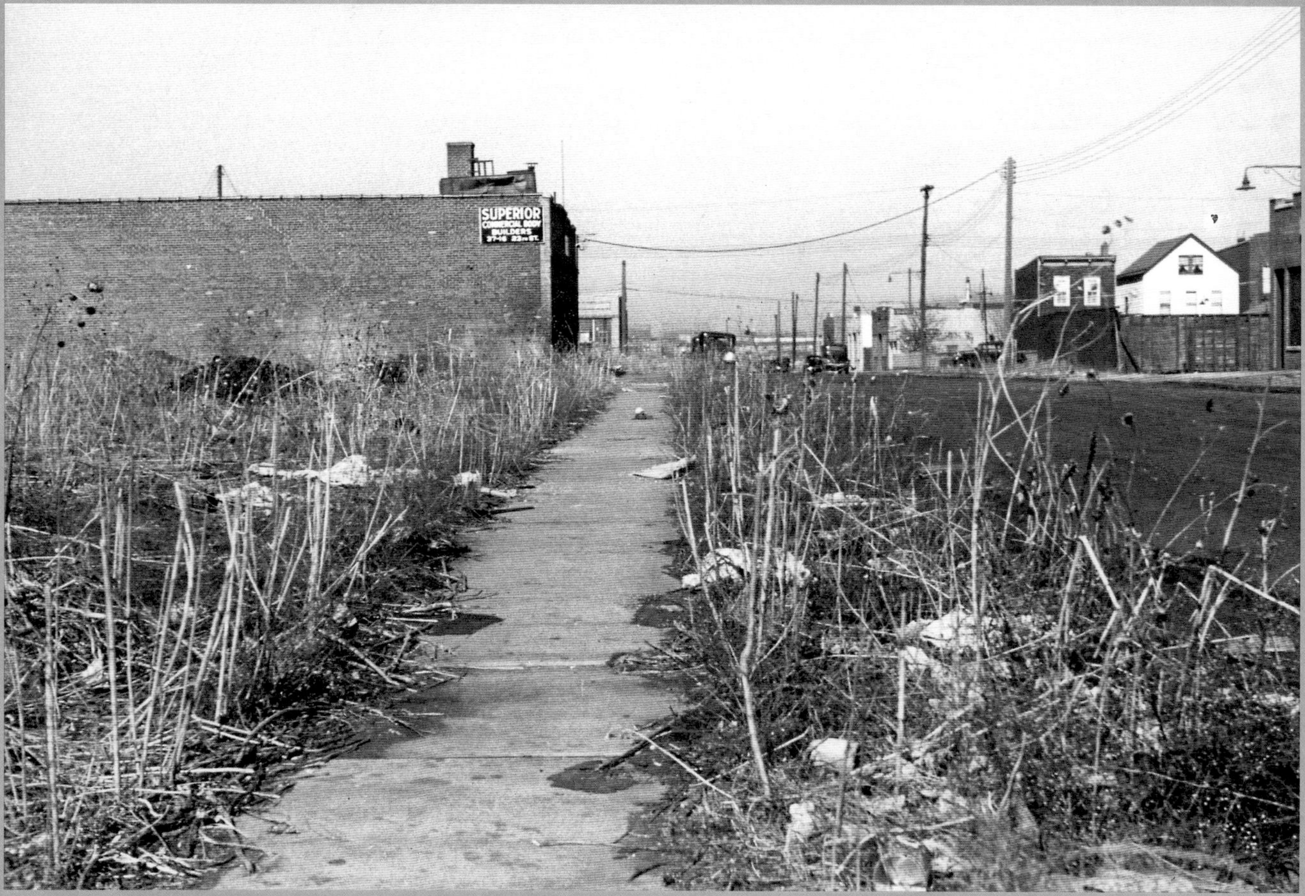
SUPERIOR
BUILDERS

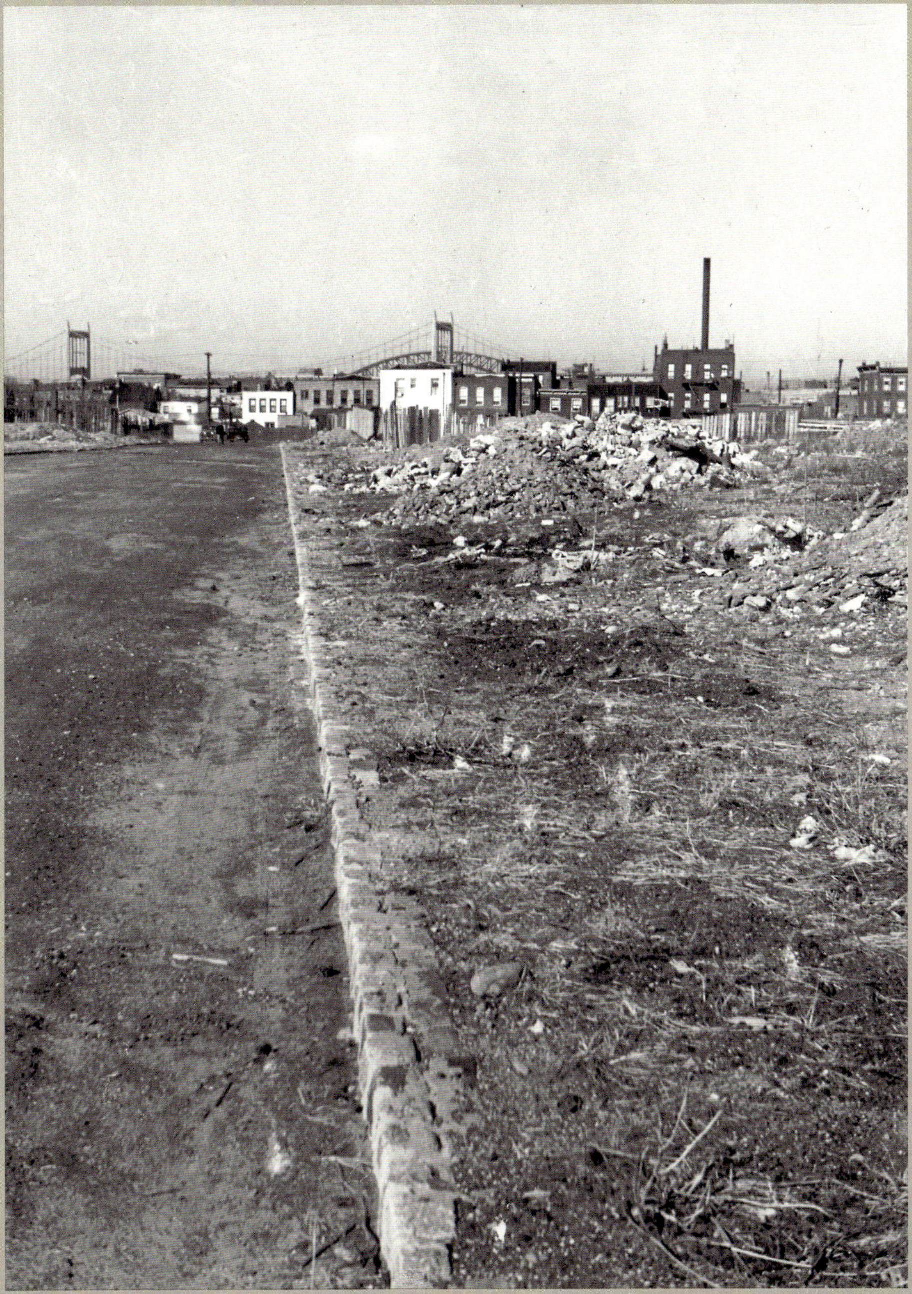

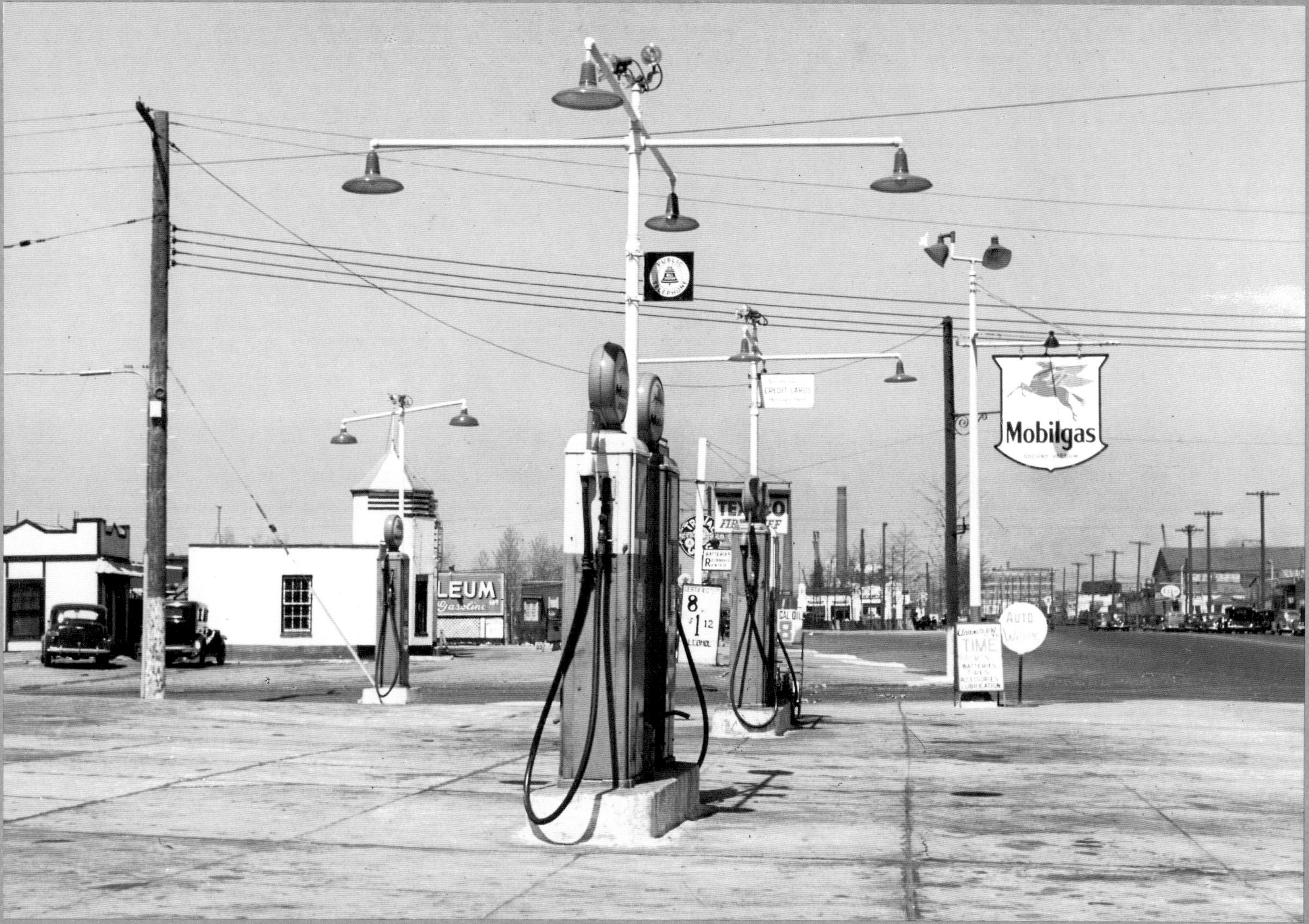
Mobilgas
LEUM
Gasoline

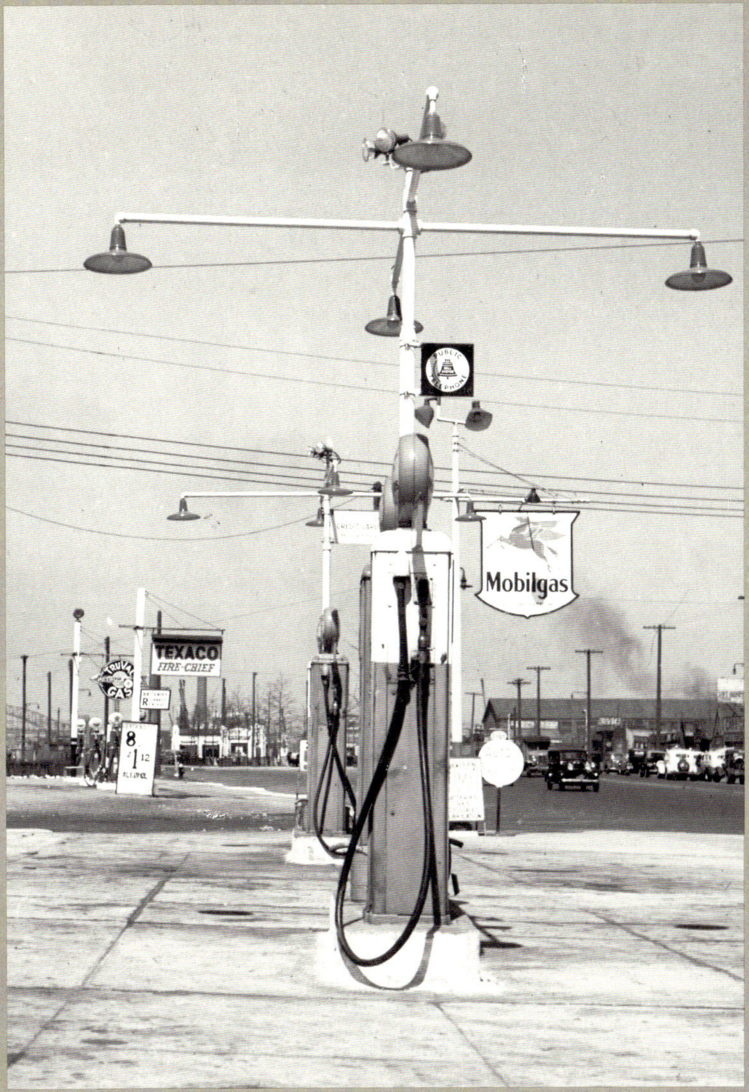
TEXACO
FIRE-CHIEF
Mobilgas

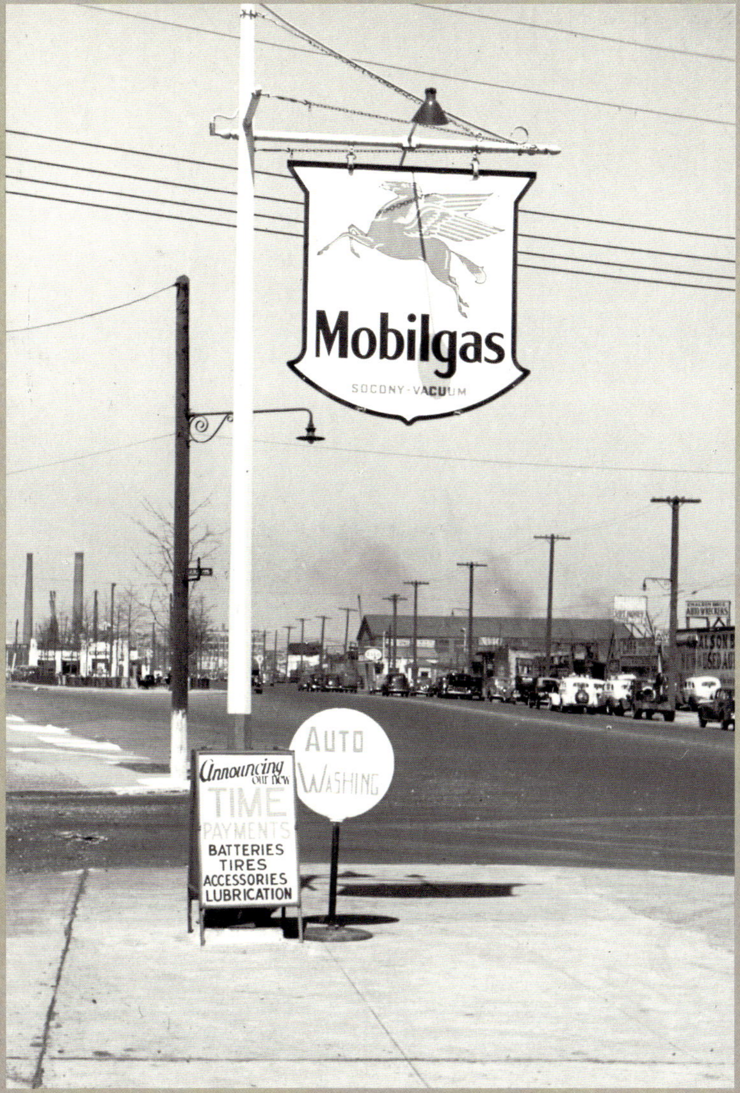
Mobilgas
SOCONY-VACUUM
Announcing our New
TIME
PAYMENTS
BATTERIES
TIRES
ACCESSORIES
LUBRICATION
AUTO
WASHING

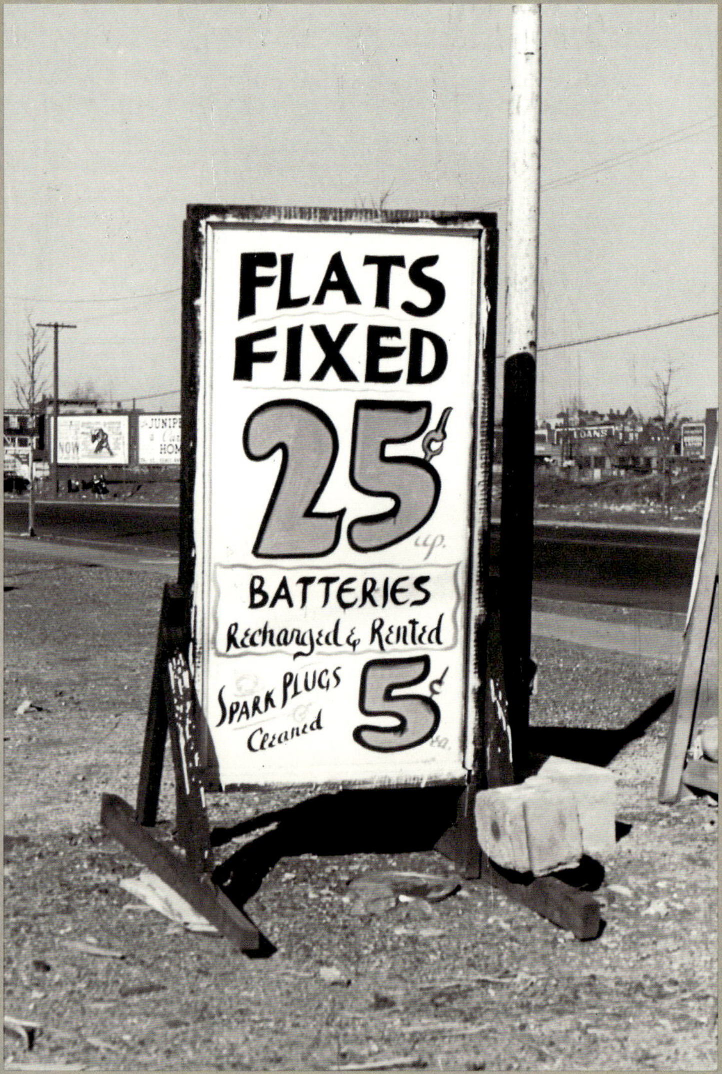
FLATS
FIXED
25¢
BATTERIES
Recharged & Rented
SPARK PLUGS
Cleaned
5¢

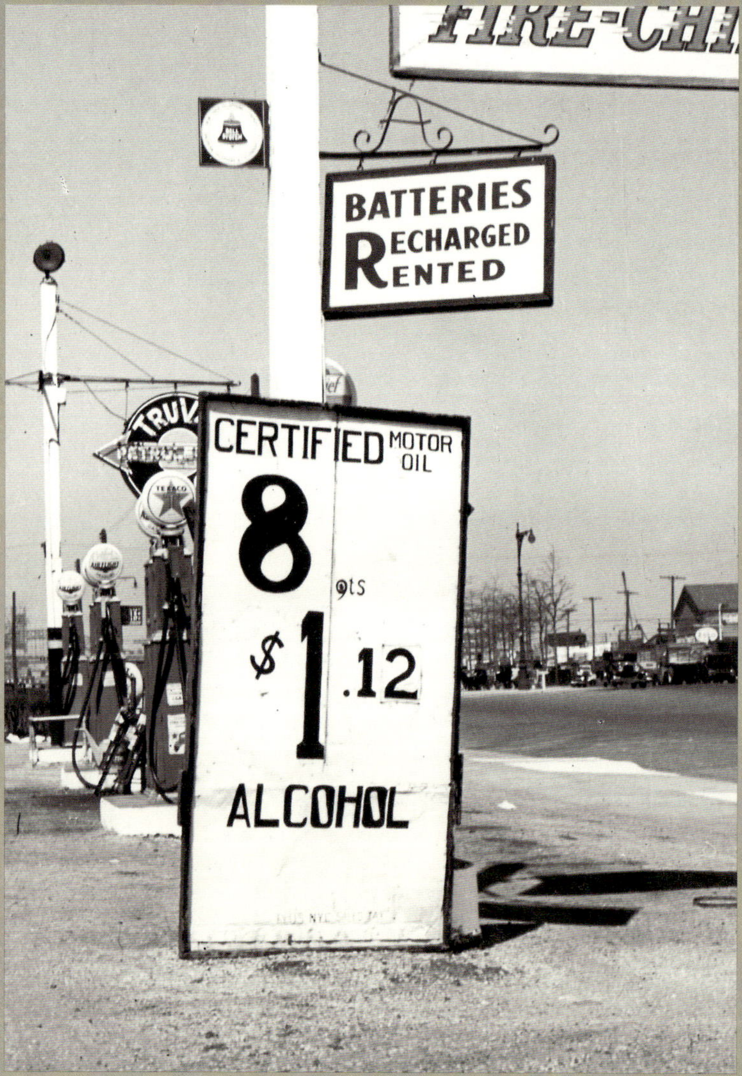
BATTERIES
RECHARGED
RENTED
CERTIFIED MOTOR OIL
8
qts
$1.12
ALCOHOL

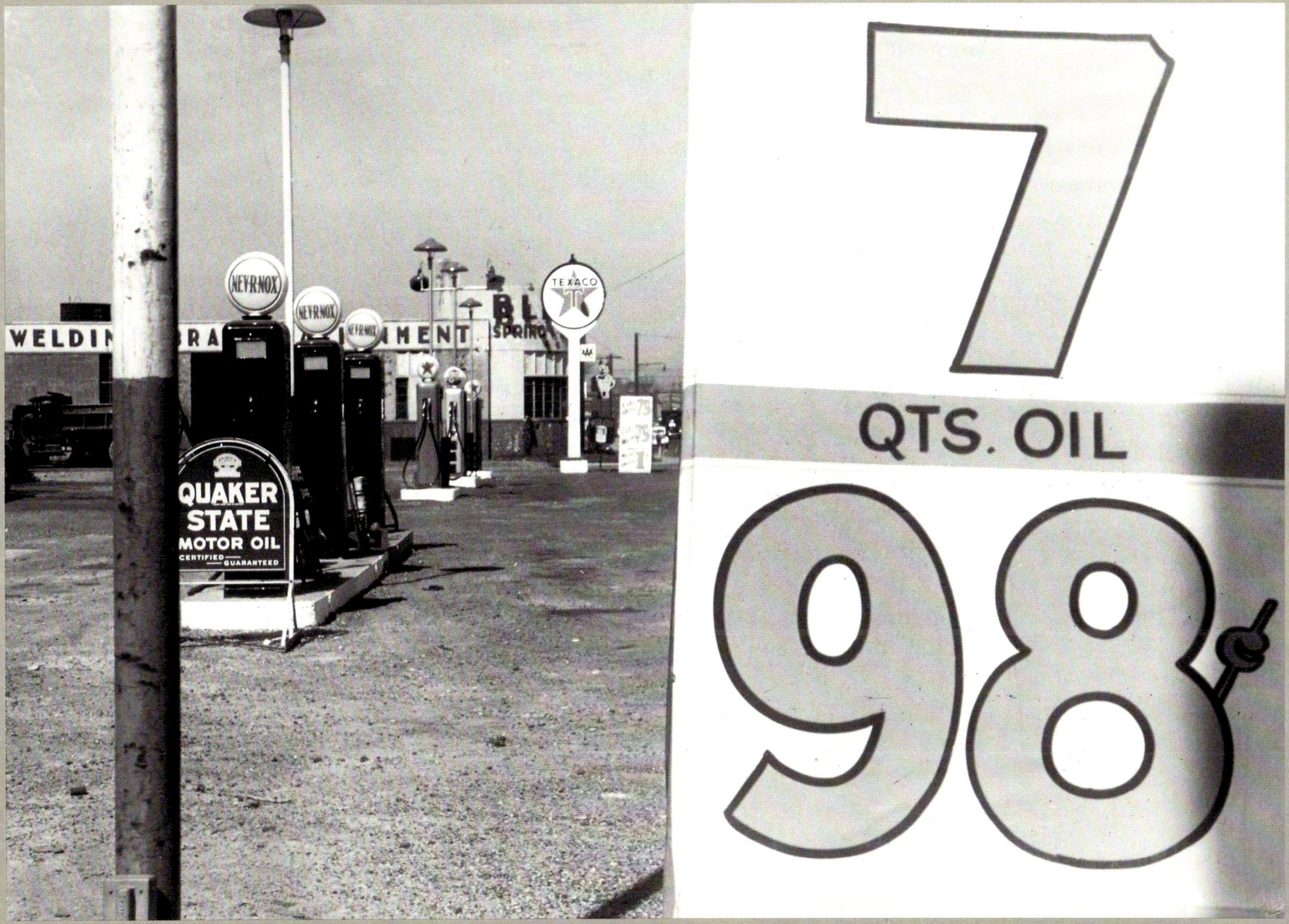
WELDIN
BRA
NMENT
NEVR-NOX
TEXACO
QUAKER STATE MOTOR OIL
CERTIFIED
GUARANTEED
7
QTS. OIL
98¢

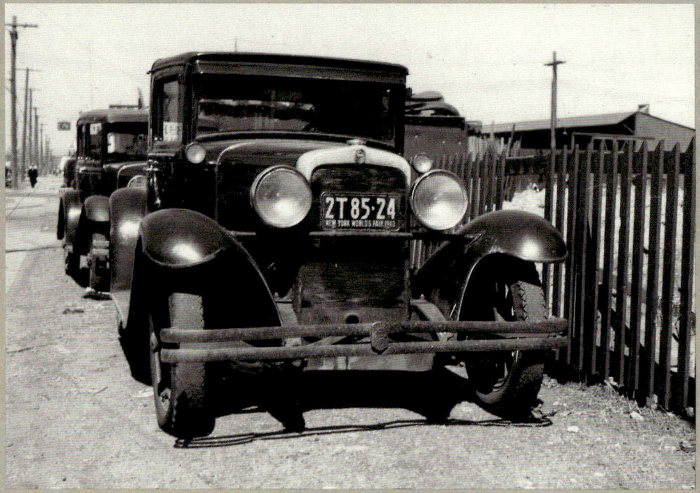
2T85·24

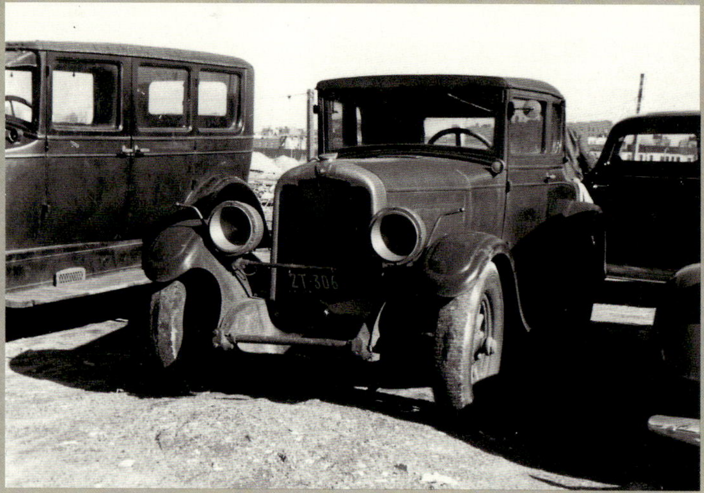
2T-306

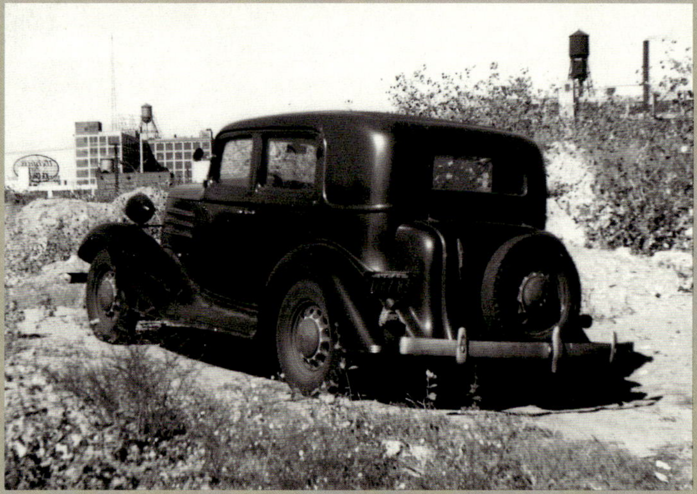

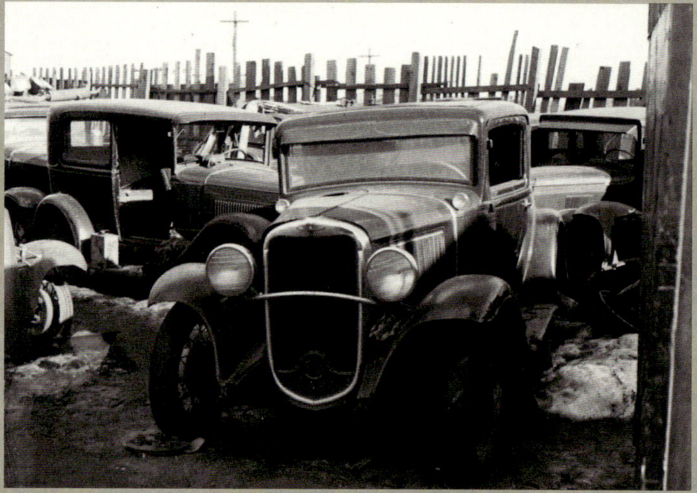

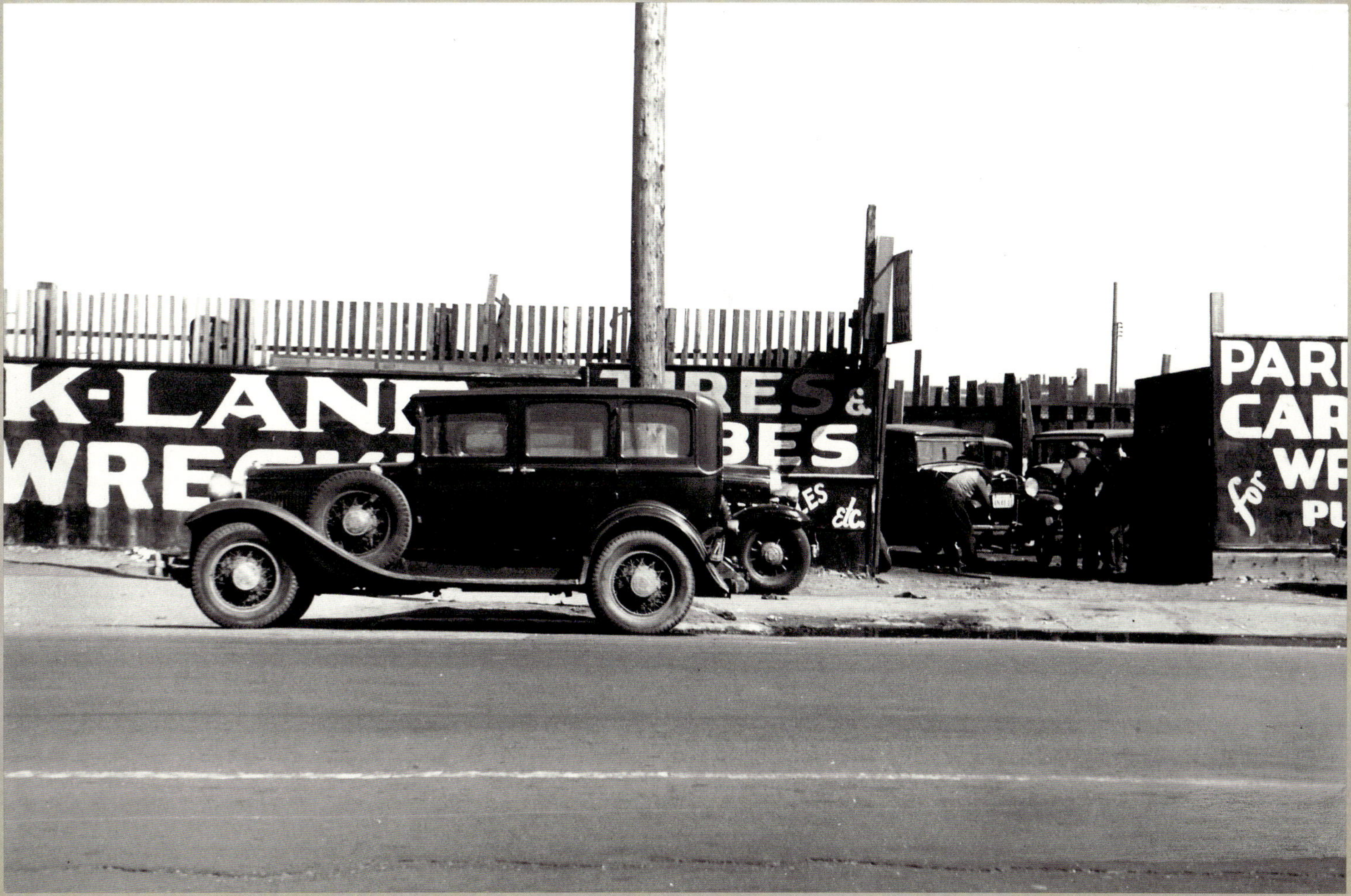
K-LAN
WREC
TIRES &
BES
ES
Etc.
PAR
CAR
for WR
PU

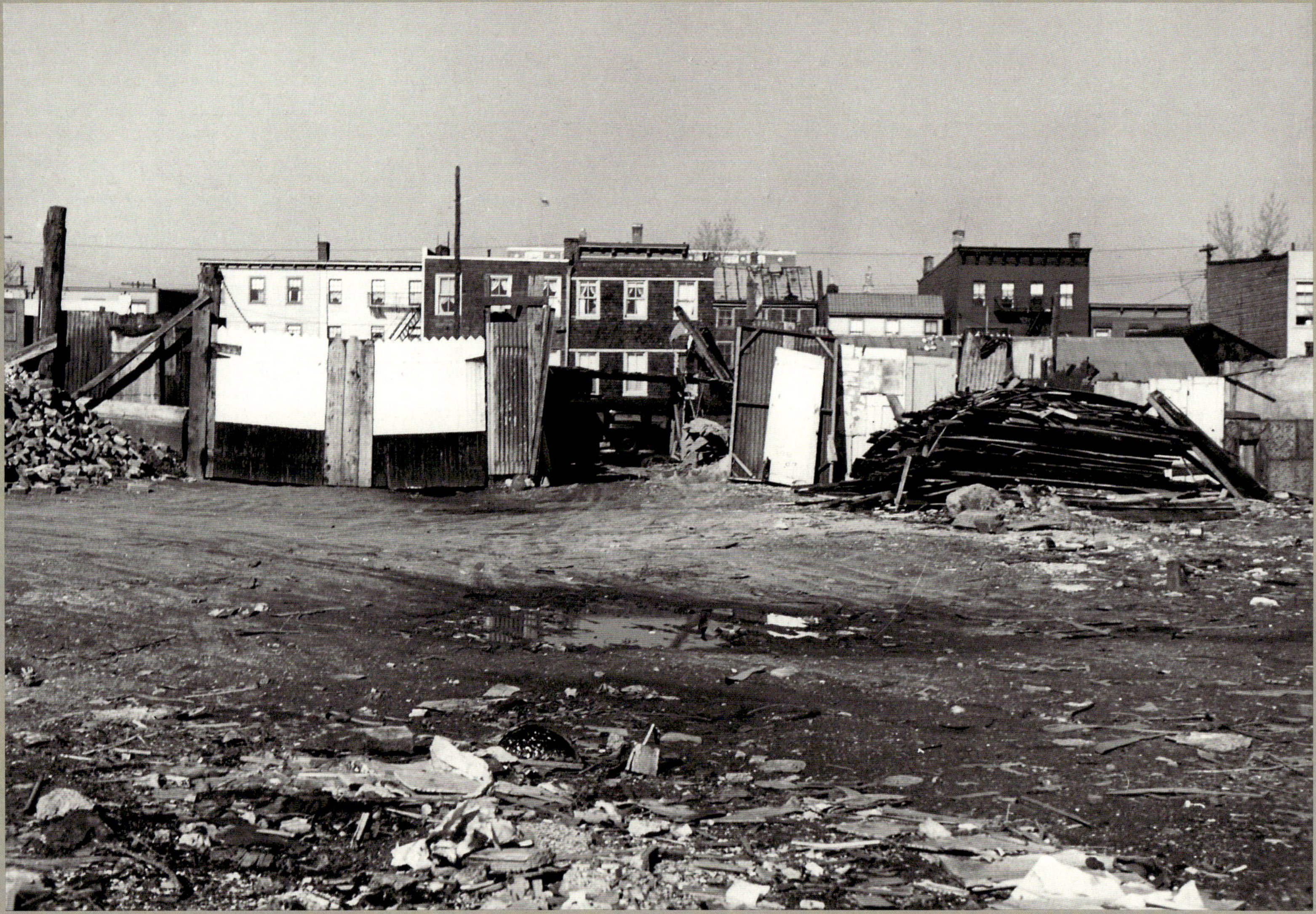

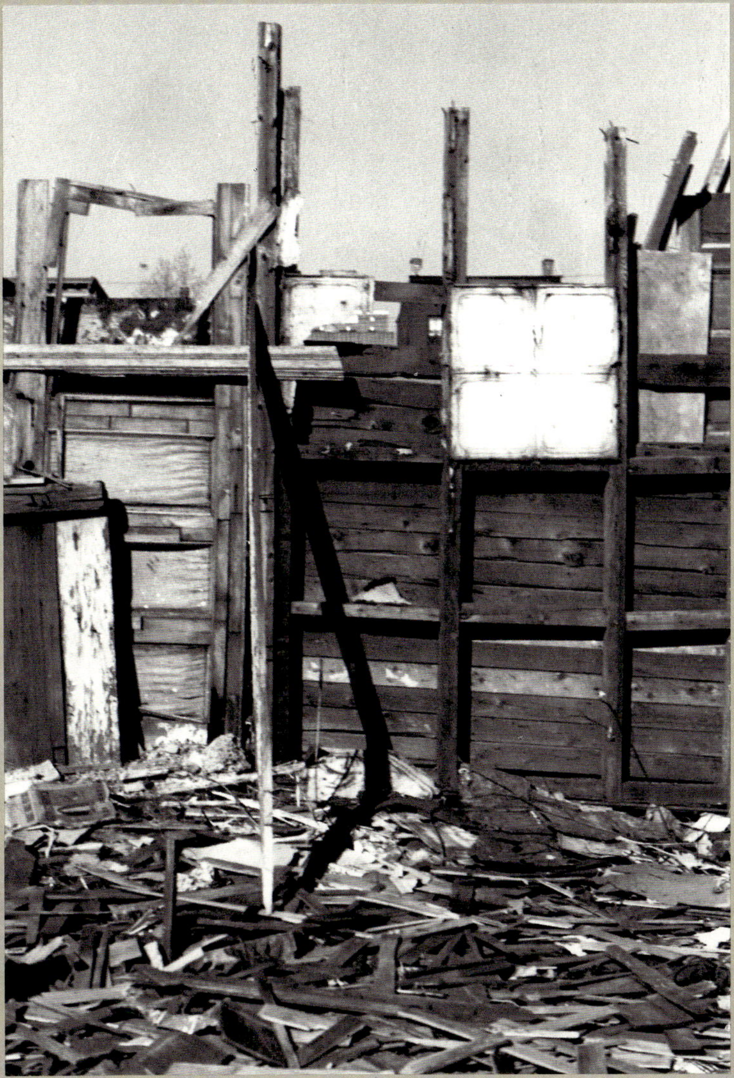

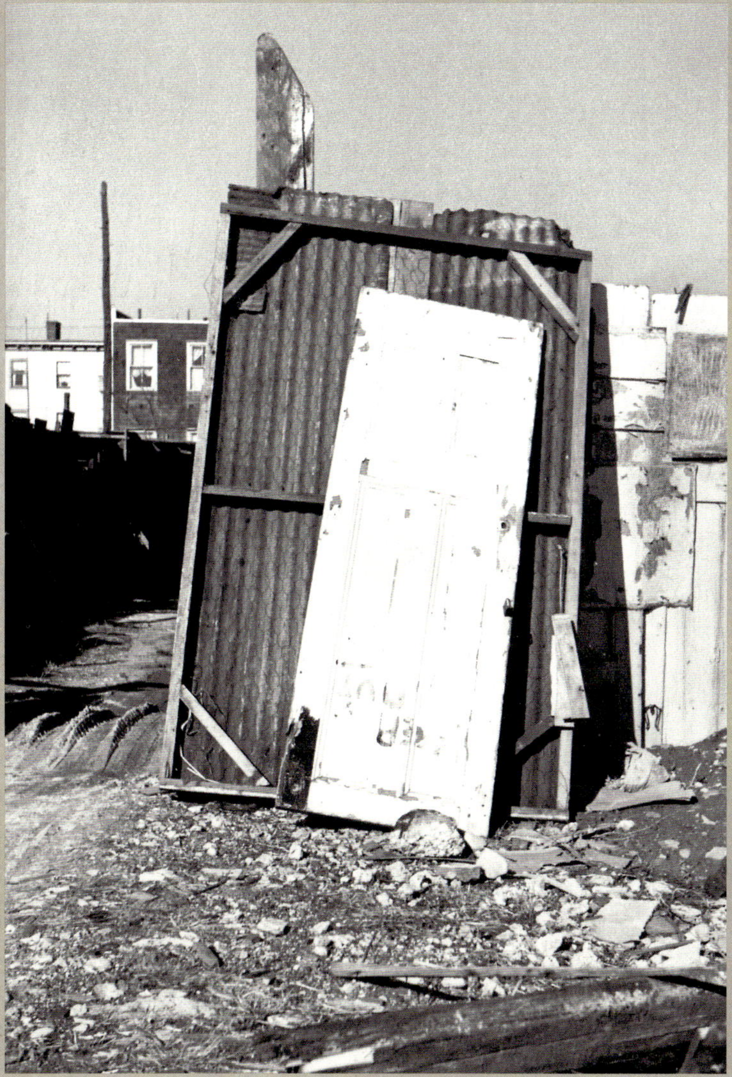

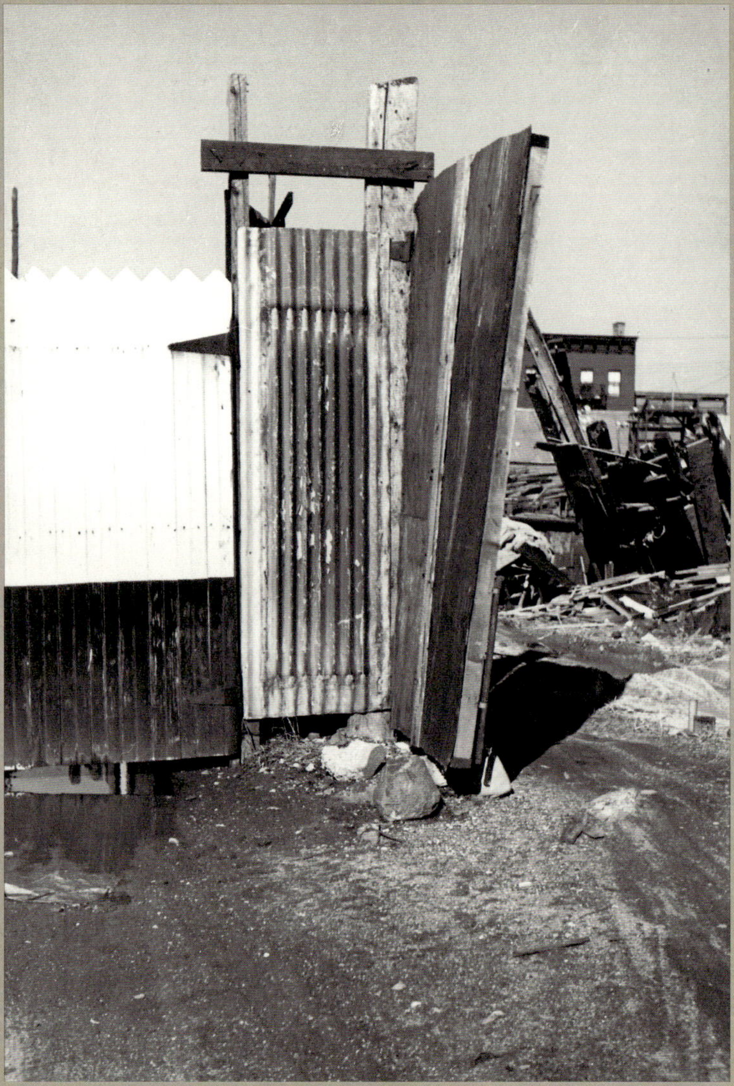

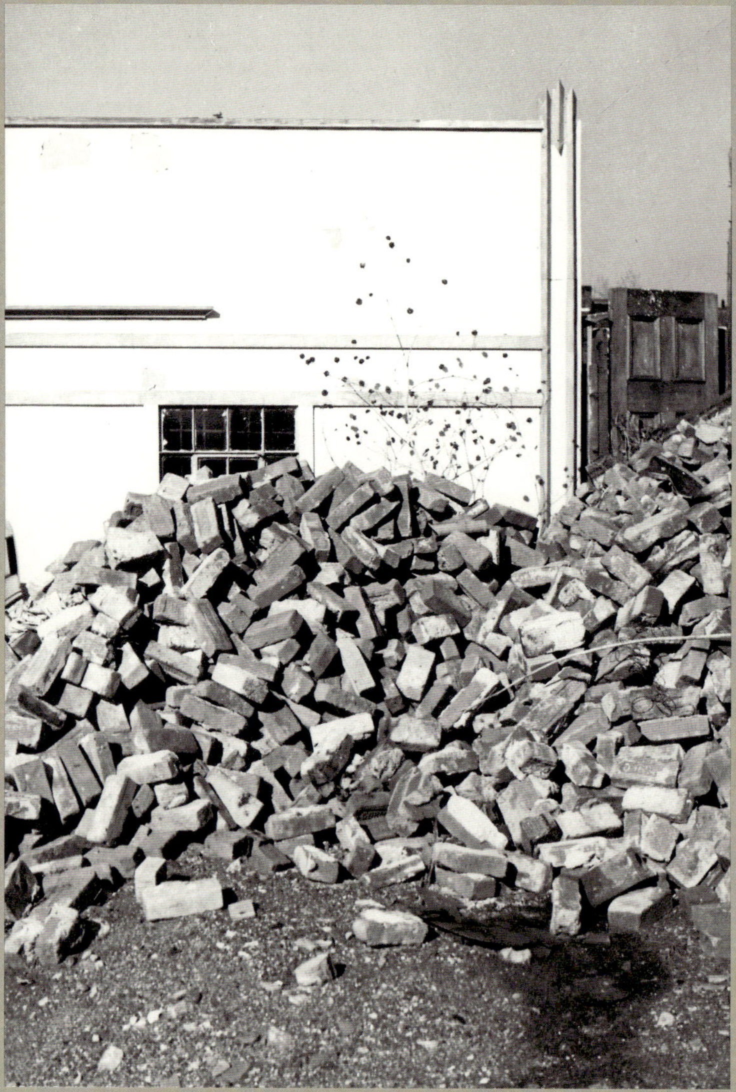

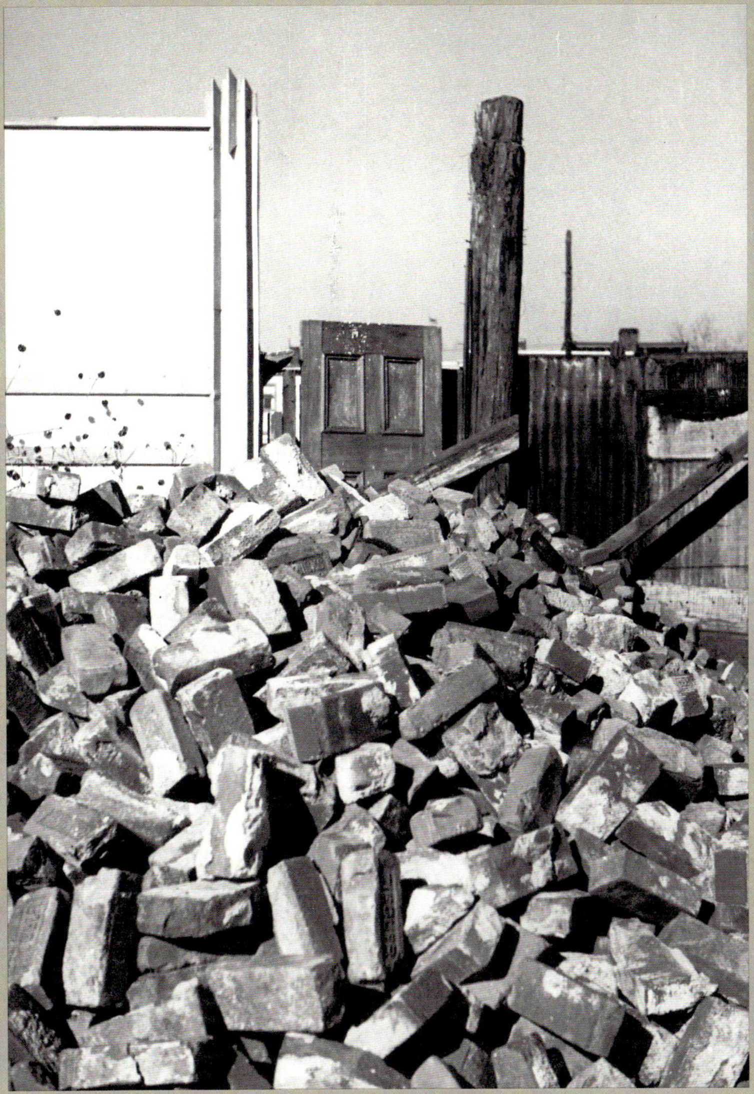

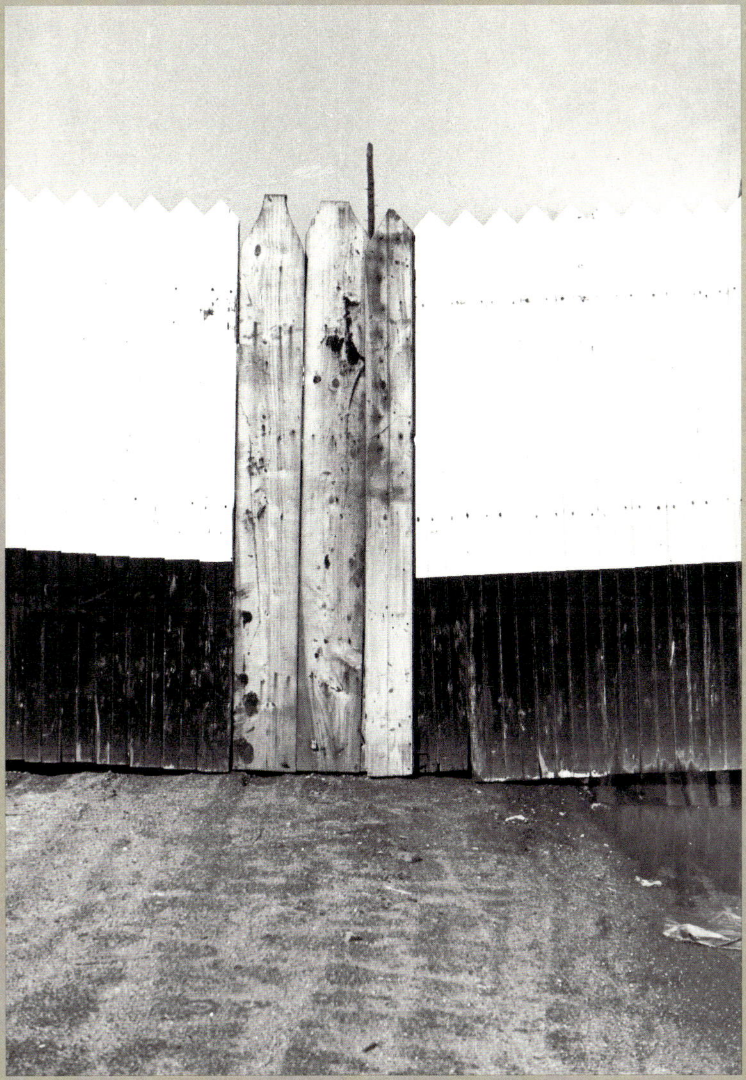

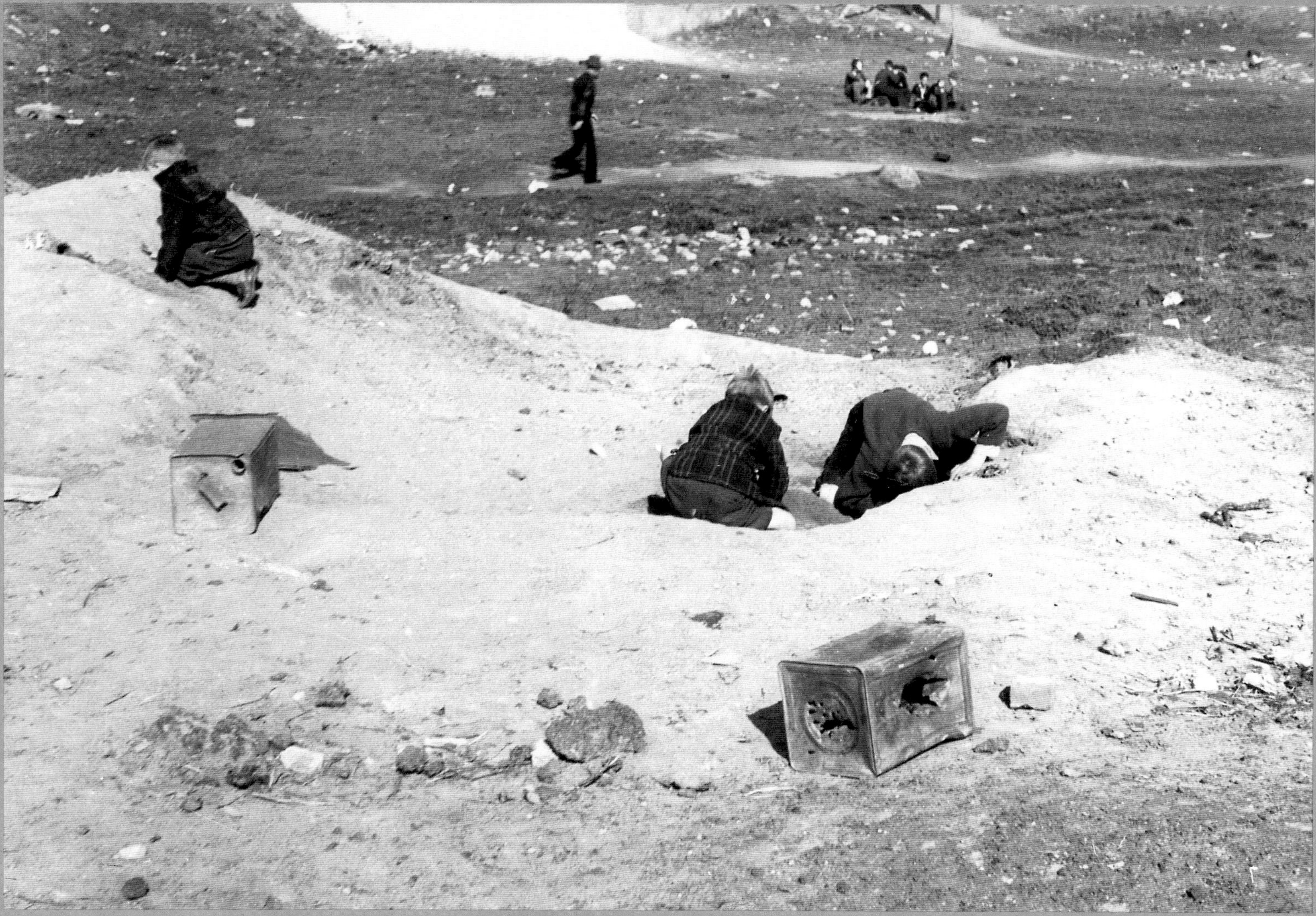

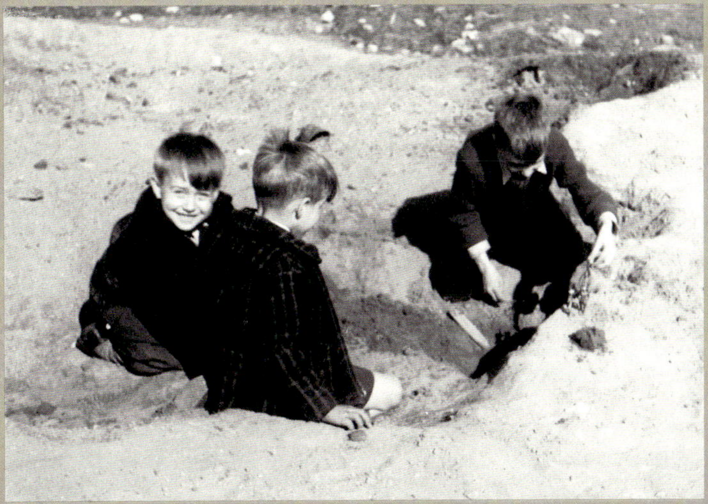
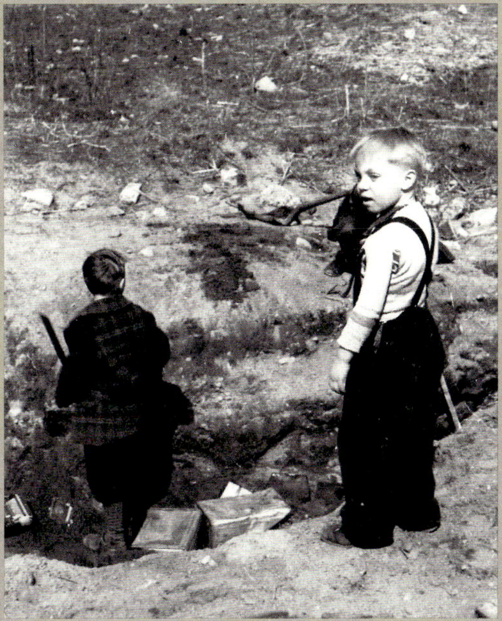
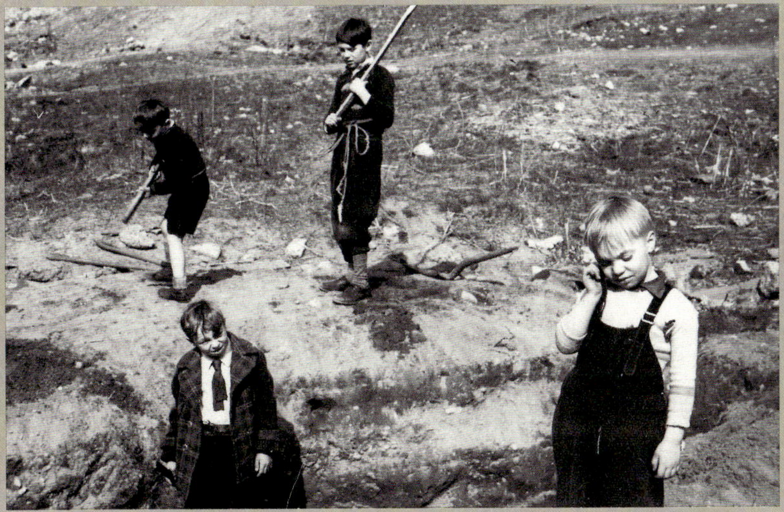
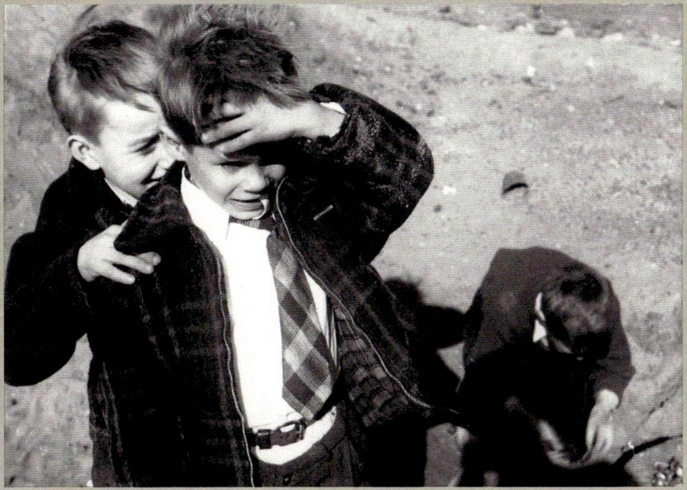

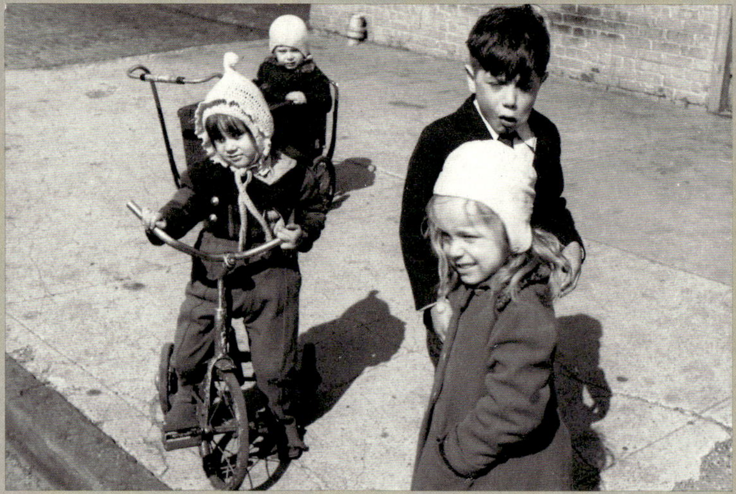
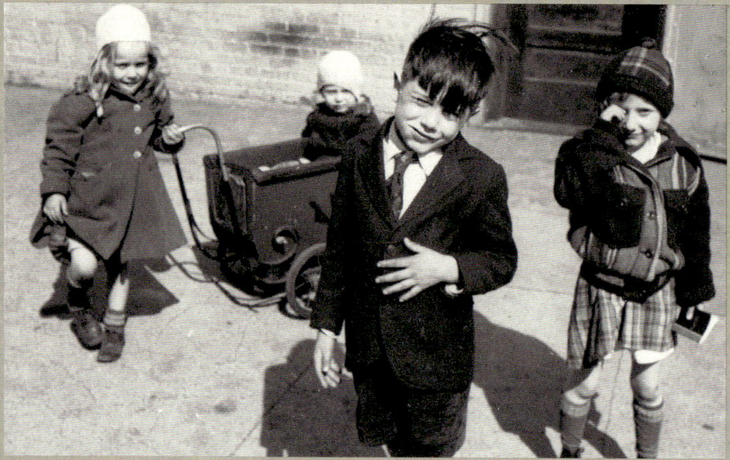
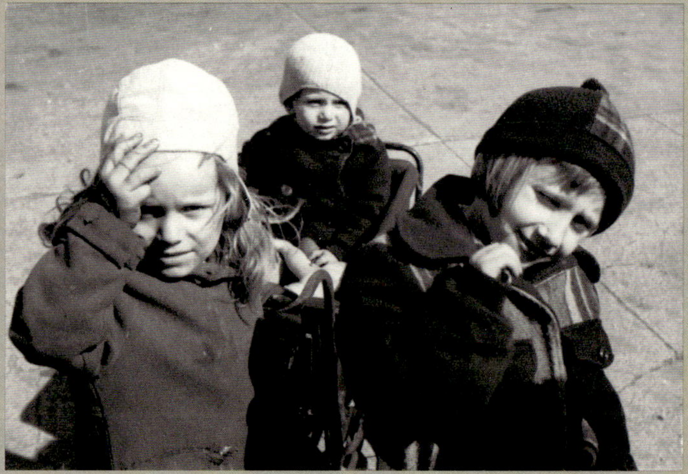
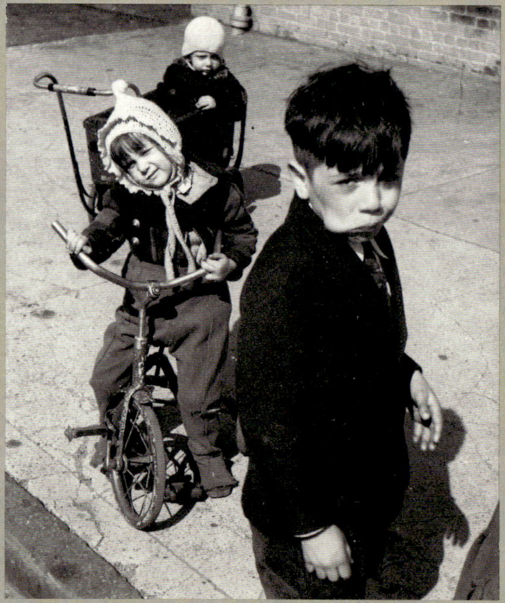

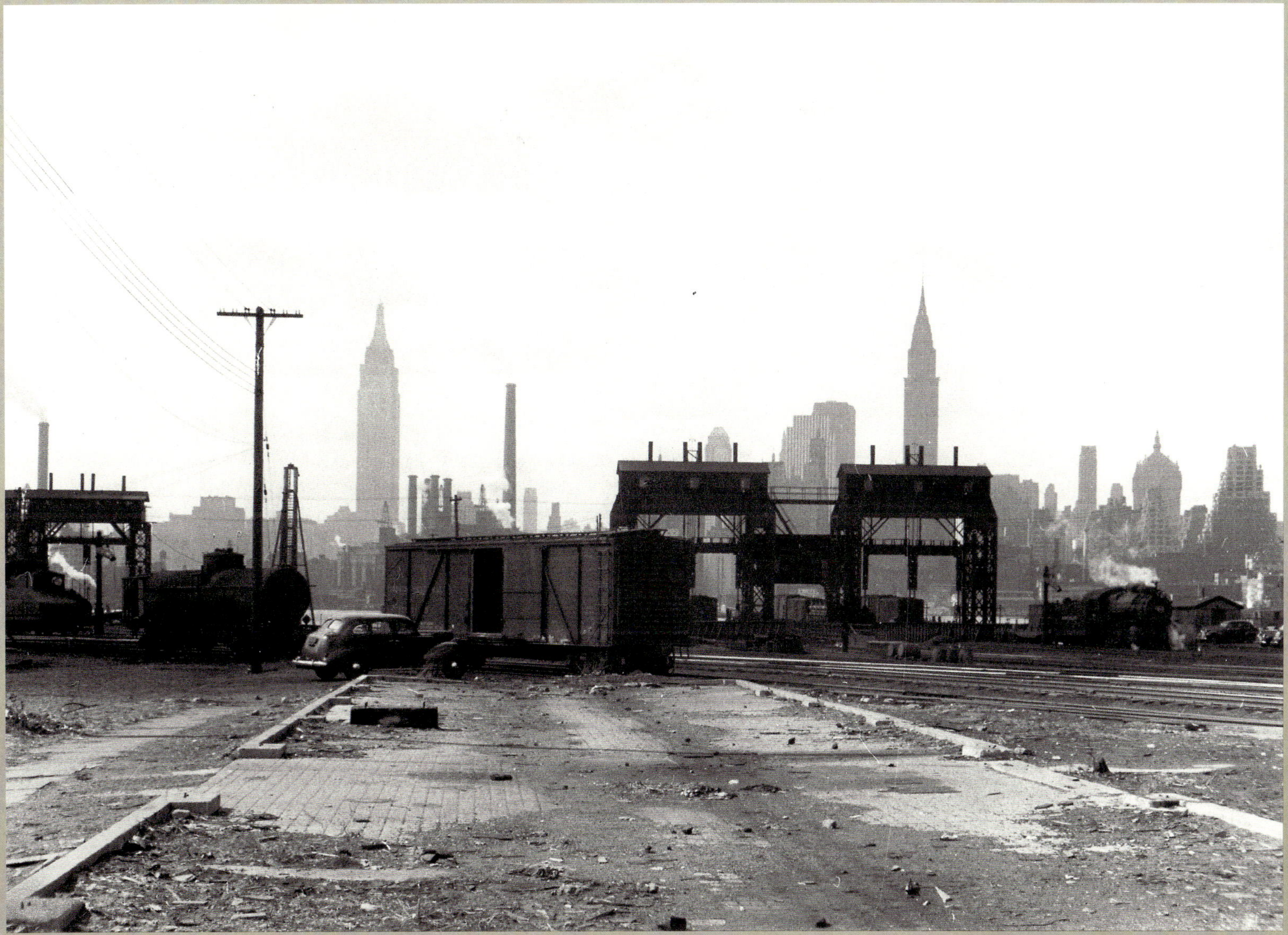

RUDY BURCKHARDT'S PLAIN POETRY

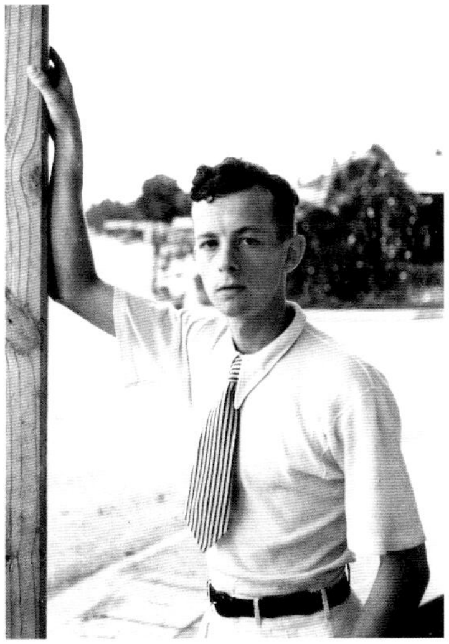

Rudy Burckhardt in Haiti, 1937–38. Photographer unknown. Collection the Estate of Rudy Burckhardt

Sarah Hermanson Meister

An Afternoon in Astoria, the words that Rudolph Burckhardt–"Rudy" became definitive much later–printed neatly in capital letters on the cover of this album, declare his modest aspirations: his subject was not the whole of his recently adopted hometown of New York City, nor the expansive borough of Queens, but an unpretentious neighborhood–and only for an afternoon. Now, more than sixty years after its creation, Burckhardt's quiet statement is virtually unknown outside a small circle of his friends and admirers. This publication is intended to capture the unassuming presentation of his original album, making his attentive, clear-eyed, often droll observations and delicate sequencing available for the first time to a broader public.

For Burckhardt, Queens was a place to escape the incessant bustle of Manhattan–a good place for his photographs and films. He later remarked, "I find it's a great place to walk because you get away from everything, and there's all kinds of things to look at. It's very quiet and spread out."[1] The borough's position just outside the center resonated with Burckhardt's sense of himself as a foreigner in New York. Wherever he worked, his photographs and films reflect his inclination to take things as they came, without judgment or sentimentality. Although Burckhardt had photographed in the metropolitan centers of London and Paris as a young man, he was "overwhelmed by [the] grandeur and ceaseless energy" of New York when he arrived here from his native Switzerland in 1935. He would recall, "The tremendous difference in scale between the soaring buildings and the people moving against them in the street astonished me, and it took a couple of years before I felt ready to photograph."[2] Burckhardt's first photographs in Manhattan are shy downward glances at sidewalks, hydrants, and signs, and at people, also seen frequently from the waist down, absorbed in their own routines. A few years later he faced the neighborhood of Astoria with straightforward confidence and care.

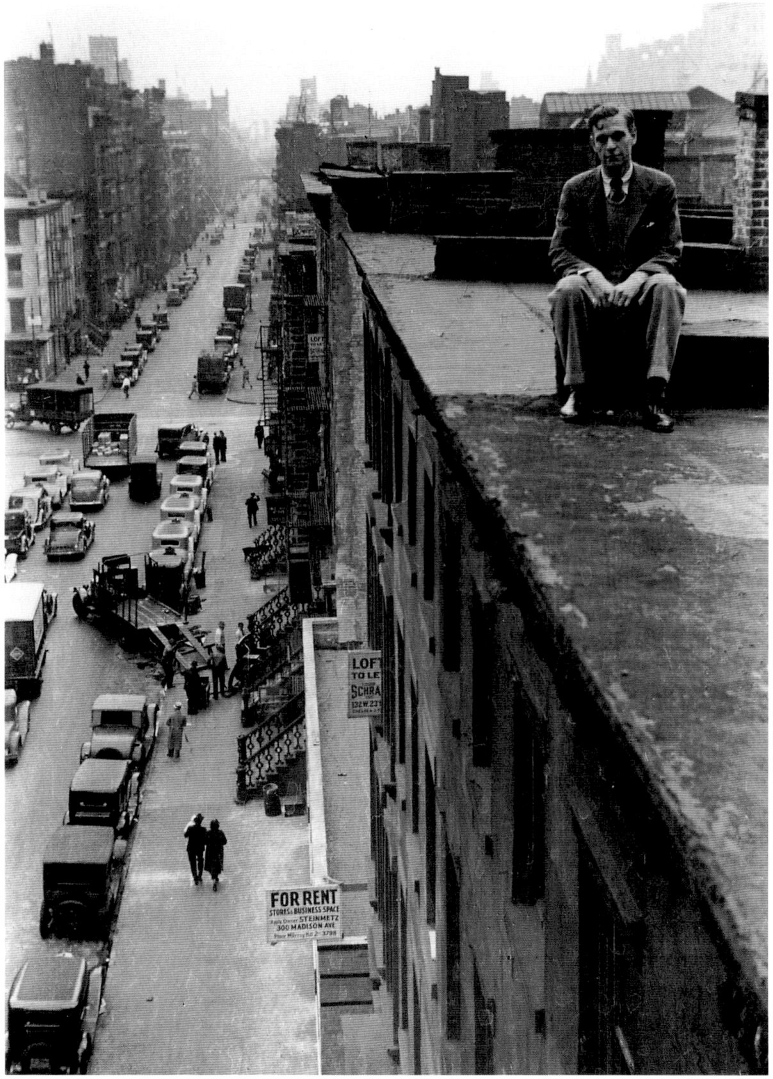

Rudy Burckhardt. **Edwin Denby on 21st Street, New York**. 1937.
Gelatin silver print, 10$\frac{3}{4}$ x 7$\frac{15}{16}$" (27.3 x 20.1 cm). Collection the Estate of Rudy Burckhardt

Burckhardt was born into an aristocratic, intellectually distinguished family in, as he described it, "proper and clean" Basel in 1914.[3] His great-great-uncle was Jacob Burckhardt, the renowned historian of the Renaissance; his grandfather was a general and judge; and his father was a prominent industrialist who died when Rudolph was fourteen. Burckhardt escaped from the weight of the past and the propriety of Europe with the help of an inheritance from his father that he came into at the age of twenty-one. Leaving for New York City, he moved into a loft at 145 West 21st Street with the poet and dance critic Edwin Denby, whom he had met in Basel the previous year, and who was to become his closest life-long friend. In New York, Burckhardt immersed himself in a culturally sophisticated bohemian life-style, and in a circle of friends encompassing artists, actors, poets, painters, musicians, filmmakers, and writers, including the young Willem de Kooning, a next-door neighbor. His first marriage, to the painter Edith Schoss, lasted fifteen years. In 1964 he married Yvonne Jacquette, also a painter, and they remained together until his suicide in 1999.

Surrounded by talent and ambition, Burckhardt was indifferent to public recognition, let alone fame. That indifference gave him room to breathe artistically, and his work flourished for decades in relative obscurity. His uncompetitive nature, combined with his refined aesthetic sense, also made him an attractive collaborator, and he made films with artists and poets across several generations, including Joseph Cornell, Larry Rivers, Alex Katz, Red Grooms, John Ashbery, Frank O'Hara, and Ron Padgett. Despite the unassuming manner in which he pursued his art, his accomplishments have occasionally received the critical attention they deserve: in 1987 The Museum of Modern Art organized a retrospective of his films, which was followed a decade later by a major exhibition of his photographs and paintings at the IVAM Centre Julio González in Valencia, Spain.[4]

In 1938 The Museum of Modern Art published Walker Evans's seminal sequence of images simply but boldly entitled *American Photographs.* The book's eighty-seven plates illustrated a sea change in the rules for advanced photography: the most mundane or ordinary fact could be the stuff of visual poetry. Burckhardt began photographing in New York at this precise time, and his impulse to capture unheralded aspects of daily life in New York without fuss or fanfare coincided perfectly with this newly dominant aesthetic.

Evans's *American Photographs* demonstrated that a sequence of mute descriptions could make up a poem, each image expanding, qualifying, and inflecting the rest. Burckhardt remade Evans's example to his own sensibility; *An Afternoon in Astoria* captures his delight in the uncelebrated and the everyday, and he constructs the relationships among the images mounted on the album pages as one would sequence shots in a film. Just as with Evans, each photograph is as thoughtfully considered and carefully composed as the next, but unlike Evans, Burckhardt often draws more than one image from the same subject, showing it at different distances and from varying points of view. He moves the viewer on in this series of unembellished and unblinking vignettes through his orchestration of the sequence and through the relative emphases established by the images' size and their number on the page. Burckhardt also appreciated this kind of control in his films, but from a viewer's perspective, an album allows the luxury of being able to linger on a particular image at will, as well as the liberty of turning back to return to previous pages to examine details and parallels that initially might have been overlooked.

Burckhardt made several films during his first years in New York, many of them comedies in which his friends played the leading roles. In *The Pursuit of Happiness*, which he made in 1940, the hustle and bustle of New York and its inhabitants are for the first time the subject rather than the backdrop, and he was simultaneously paying increased attention to the city in his still photography. The playfulness of his unscripted comedies carries over, manifesting itself in his experimentation with montage and split screens, camera rotation and manipulation of film speed. Burckhardt made this short silent film just before he was drafted into the U.S. Army (although he was not yet a citizen) and stationed in Trinidad for "three inglorious years."[5] It wasn't long before he was exploring even closer relationships between his films and his photographic work; most of the footage in *The Climate of New York* (1948) is taken directly from his still photographs—the same ones that had inspired Denby to write the sonnets he read as voice-overs in the film.

The tender curiosity in *Under the Brooklyn Bridge* (1953) is the closest approximation of *An Afternoon in Astoria* in moving pictures. Choosing another off-the-beaten-path locale, Burckhardt pursues his unglamorous subject without condescension, delicately capturing the nuances of work and life in the neighborhood under the Brooklyn Bridge. Music by Debussy and Poulenc complements the scenes without directly corresponding to them. Although the film was created over a decade after *An Afternoon in Astoria*, both adopt the same seminarrative, walk-in-the-neighborhood form. The album is a virtual stepping stone between Burckhardt's still photography and his films.

Evans's *American Photographs* notwithstanding, when Burckhardt was preparing albums of his work in Queens there were few public forums for photography as personal art. Burckhardt's albums are an original invention—an attempt to give shape to the best of his work in an artistically

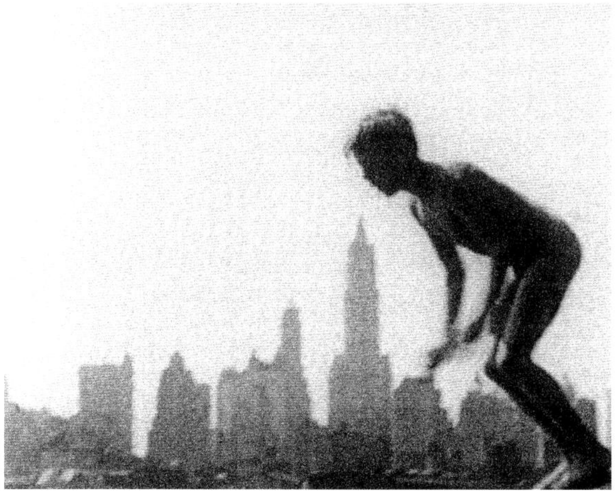

Rudy Burckhardt. **Under the Brooklyn Bridge.** 1953. Film, 16mm, black and white, 15 minutes. Collection the Estate of Rudy Burckhardt

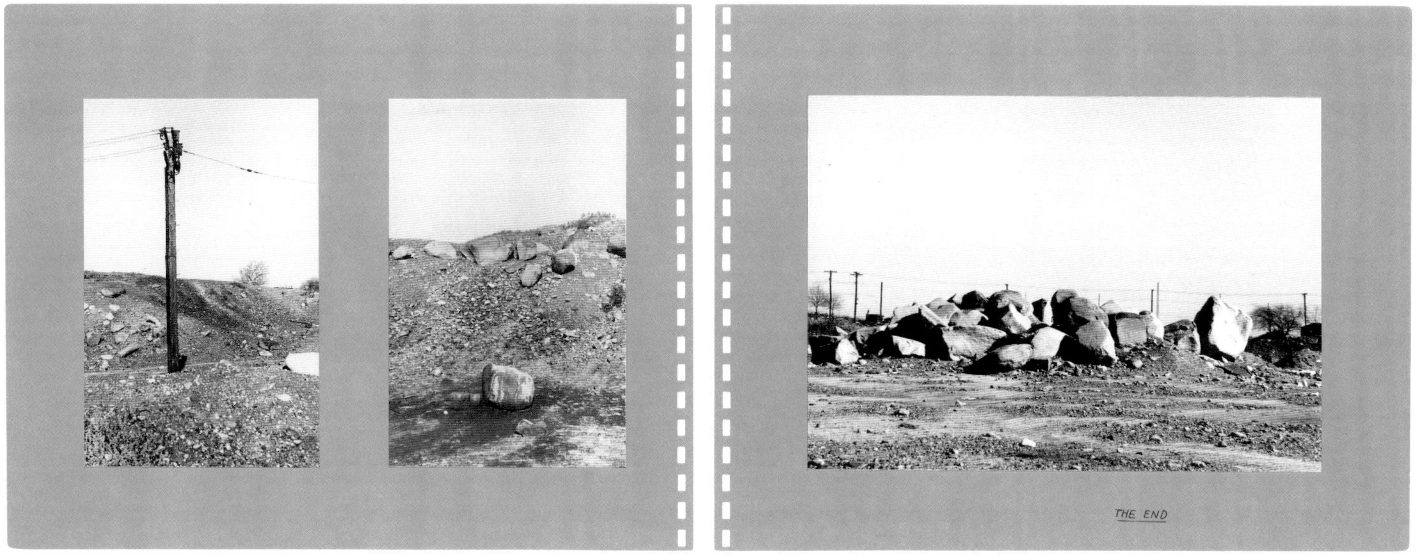

Rudy Burckhardt. **A Walk through Astoria and Other Places in Queens.** 1943. Spread from an album of gelatin silver prints, each page 9 15/16 x 13" (25.3 x 33 cm). Private collection

serious way, even though the audience consisted exclusively of himself and his family and friends. Interviewed in the early 1970s, Burckhardt remembered that he made a few of these albums (he refers to them as scrapbooks), then set them aside for decades.[6] The earliest known album, from the late 1930s, neatly divides into three chapters that focus on sidewalk architecture, storefront signage, and human activity in the streets of Manhattan. Entitled *New York, N. Why?*, this album includes several of the Denby poems that were inspired by Burckhardt's photography. *An Afternoon in Astoria* and *A Walk through Astoria and Other Places in Queens* are the only two known albums that focus on Queens. In both, Burckhardt dry-mounted the photographs on the same neutral gray board, which he spiral-bound into a book. The photographs in *An Afternoon in Astoria* were taken in 1940, those in *A Walk through Astoria and Other Places in Queens* in 1943. (The latter album also includes five of Denby's sonnets.) Although the two albums include photographs from the same terrain, no image appears in both. The subjects in each are featured in multiple views, and the size and sequence of each print are carefully considered for its relation to its neighbors and to the album as a whole.

In about 1947 Burckhardt made another album of his Manhattan photographs, which is untitled and.opens with a poem of Denby's. Here his approach to the city and its inhabitants is bolder and more direct: he ventures up to rooftops to capture an insider's view of the skyline, he delves down into the subway, and he places individuals on the streets within the context of their urban landscape. Burckhardt made three additional albums of photographs from outside New York—two of pictures mainly from Italy, in 1947 and 1951, and one of Great Spruce Head Island, off the coast of Maine, in 1952. Although more simply crafted than their predecessors, with one photograph per page, these albums elevate the notion of the travel journal, providing affectless insight into their chosen subjects.[7]

In February 1940 (a date suggested by license plates and movie posters in the photographs), Burckhardt traveled from Manhattan to Queens for perhaps a single afternoon.[8] He captured a few overall views, some gas stations and signs, a sampling of abandoned cars and neglected lots, and a handful of children playing. Burckhardt begins and ends his observations with images of streets, sidewalks and empty lots, which serve as visual bookends for the album. Telephone wires, curbs, and skylines provide compositional structure throughout, and human activity is represented largely by its artifacts: cars and buildings, signs and debris.

At the heart of *An Afternoon in Astoria* are Burckhardt's investigations of four subjects: gas stations, cars, abandoned lots, and children playing. Each subject is depicted across a sequence of images—most often an overall opening shot followed by details, although this rhythm is occasionally subverted. The album opens with a series of images of vacant lots and empty streets. The first gas station view is wide enough to include several adjacent operations, whose pumps, lights, and signage overlap most densely in the center of the image; subsequent photographs are close-ups focusing on placards offering various automotive remedies. The last gas station image distills these formal choices into one: a close view of an oil advertisement (seven quarts of oil for ninety-eight cents!) occupies the right side of the image and is balanced against a view of gas pumps receding at a comfortable distance on the left.

These spreads are followed by one on cars, beginning on the left with four small photographs mounted on the same page, so that the eye bumps from one to the next as in the jump cuts of a film. It finds rest on the full-page image opposite, which shows an auto-body yard with a car parked outside. Only here, more than halfway through the album, do people appear for the first time. Small figures in the shadows, they are dwarfed by cars and fences, and they face away from the camera, unaware of and indifferent to Burckhardt's presence. Instead they focus on a car in duress, like those on the previous page–and the future of all of these vehicles seems even more uncertain after we make out the letters "WRECK" in big letters along the body-yard fence. If all of the automobiles in Astoria were in this state, there would be little need for the gas stations pictured on the previous pages; clearly Burckhardt chose these cars over more functional ones, and their isolation and disrepair contribute to the mood he has established with the scenes of emptiness and neglect in his first images.

The following page features a single image of an abandoned lot teeming with scraps, dilapidated fences, weeds, and rubble, which is succeeded by six details, mounted evenly two to a page. The subjects–piles of bricks, leaning fences–become increasingly nondescript, evoking a mood, but the series of images as a whole tells us no more about the objects in them than a single image would; instead, careful structural repetitions draw our attention to the visual relationships that Burckhardt has so conscientiously crafted and preserved, encouraging us to consider the album for its form as well as its content. Children are the focus of the album's last group of scenes: first an overall view of a hilly, forsaken lot with children scattered about, some of them in Sunday clothes, then four details of children playing in it, and finally four images of children on the sidewalk. Burckhardt held his photographs to high standards; each one had to be "perfect in terms of interest everywhere."[9] Even when they are mounted four to a page, a viewer is rewarded for examining each one individually.

Although none of Denby's poems is included in *An Afternoon in Astoria*, an entire section of the anthology *Edwin Denby: The Complete Poems* is titled "Poems Written to Accompany Photographs by Rudy Burckhardt."[10] The first of his "Five Reflections" resonates with this album, putting forth in words the plain poetry of Burckhardt's photographs:

Hung Sundays from Manhattan by the spacious
59th Street Bridge are the clear afternoons
In Astoria and other open places
Further in the enormous borough of Queens.

Thickly settled plain an ocean climate cleans
Rail and concrete, asphalt and weed oasis,
Remote Queens constructs like desert-landscape scenes
Vacant sky, vacant lots, a few Sunday faces.

In this backyard of exploitation and refuse
Chance vistas, weights in the air part and compose–
Curbs, a cloud, metropolitan bulks for use
Caught off guard distend and balance and repose.

So New York photographed without distortions
Show we walk among noble proportions.

This album is published on the occasion of the opening of MoMA QNS, The Museum of Modern Art's new facility in Queens, in June 2002. Rudy Burckhardt was here, more than sixty years ago, and for more than an afternoon.

NOTES

1. Rudy Burckhardt, quoted in Simon Pettet, *Conversations with Rudy Burckhardt about Everything* (New York: Vehicle Editions, 1987), n.p.
2. Burckhardt, "Escritos," in *Rudy Burckhardt* (Valencia: IVAM Centre Julio González, 1998), p. 194.
3. Burckhardt, quoted in Vincent Katz, "Mobile Homes: The Art of Rudy Burckhardt," in ibid., p. 186.
4. In addition to the 1998 catalogue accompanying the IVAM exhibition, which includes essays by Katz and Robert Storr as well as a filmography, recent publications of Burckhardt's work include Burckhardt and Pettet, *Talking Pictures: The Photography of Rudy Burckhardt* (Cambridge, Mass.: Zoland Books, 1994), and Burckhardt and Katz, *Boulevard Transportation* (New York: Tibor de Nagy Editions, 1997), as well as a twenty-four-page insert in *Parkett* no. 48 (December 1996). Burckhardt collaborated with Edwin Denby on two books: *In Public, In Private* (Prairie City, Ill.: Decker Press, 1948) and *Mediterranean Cities* (New York: George Wittenborn, 1956), and has also published *Mobile Homes*, a book of his memoirs and selected writings (Calais, Vermont: Z Press, 1979).
5. See Burckhardt, "Escritos," p. 195.
6. "I pasted [my early photographs] in scrapbooks with [Denby's] poems interspersed, and then put them away. Last year, two young poets, Ron Padgett and Larry Fagin, asked to see my early photos, and I showed them the scrapbooks." Burckhardt, quoted in Grace Glueck, "Back to 5-Cent Malted and Plenty of Room to Stroll," *New York Times*, March 13, 1972.
7. *New York, N. Why?* is in the collection of the Metropolitan Museum of Art, New York. *An Afternoon in Astoria* and the untitled album of Manhattan photographs are in the collection of The Museum of Modern Art. The other Queens album is held in a private collection, and the albums of Italy and Maine are currently at the Tibor de Nagy Gallery, New York, courtesy of the Estate of Rudy Burckhardt.
8. We cannot be certain that all of the album's images were taken in a single afternoon, as Burckhardt's title suggests, but it seems likely. A virtually cloudless sky appears in image after image, and the cold, clear light that casts crisp, dark shadows is consistent throughout the album.
9. Burckhardt, quoted in Martica Swain, Oral History Interview, Smithsonian Archives of American Art, January 14, 1993. The text is available online at http://artarchives.si.edu/oralhist/burckh93.htm.
10. Edwin Denby, *Edwin Denby: The Complete Poems*, ed. and with an introduction by Ron Padgett and with essays by Frank O'Hara and Lincoln Kirstein (New York: Random House, 1986), p. 78.

BURCKHARDT'S ALBUMS

Rudy Burckhardt made at least seven albums of his photographs, all black and white gelatin silver prints.

In the dimensions, height precedes width.

New York, N. Why? c. 1939

$11\frac{5}{16}$ x $12\frac{13}{16}$" (28.7 x 32.5 cm)

67 photographs mounted on 25 sheets of light-weight off-white card. Cover an additional 2 sheets of a thicker stock

In three sections, titled "Part 1," "Part 2," "Part 3."

Includes six typed sonnets by Edwin Denby and one typed quotation from an article by Denby in *The New Yorker* magazine

The Metropolitan Museum of Art, New York. Purchase, Estate of Florence Waterbury

An Afternoon in Astoria. 1940

$9\frac{15}{16}$ x 13" (25.3 x 33 cm)

35 photographs mounted on 11 sheets of gray card, including cover of the same stock

The Museum of Modern Art, New York. Gift of CameraWorks, Inc., and Purchase

A Walk through Astoria and Other Places in Queens. 1943

$9\frac{15}{16}$ x 13" (25.3 x 33 cm)

71 photographs mounted on 25 sheets of gray card, including cover of the same stock

With one subsection, titled "Laurel Hill."

Includes five typed sonnets by Edwin Denby, with some corrections in pencil

Private collection

Untitled (Manhattan). 1946–47

$10\frac{1}{4}$ x $12\frac{3}{16}$" (26 x 31 cm)

28 photographs, some printed 2 to a page, and mounted back-to-back to form 13 sheets, including front cover of a similar stock

Incomplete: the album lacks a back cover, and Burckhardt is said to have removed some pages.

Includes one typed sonnet by Edwin Denby

The Museum of Modern Art, New York. Gift of CameraWorks, Inc., and Purchase

Untitled (Italy). 1947

10 x $7\frac{15}{16}$" (25.4 x 20.2 cm)

36 photographs mounted back-to-back to form 22 sheets, some without images, including cover of same stock

The photographs appear under the following headings: Firenze (3), Siena (11), Toscana (7), Arezzo (3), Perugia (3), Ancona (3), and Ravenna (5). On the cover is a photograph that Burckhardt elsewhere titled *Piazza, Milan* (1947)

Tibor de Nagy Gallery, New York. Courtesy the Estate of Rudolph Burckhardt

Untitled (Italy and Greece). 1951

$9\frac{15}{16}$ x $8\frac{1}{16}$" (25.2 x 20.5 cm)

26 photographs mounted back-to-back to form 19 sheets, some without images. Cover an additional 2 sheets of a thicker stock

The photographs appear under the following headings: Florence (1), Rome (5), Marino (1), Venice (9), Sicily (5), Greece (5)

Tibor de Nagy Gallery, New York. Courtesy the Estate of Rudolph Burckhardt

Great Spruce Head Island. 1952

10 x $7\frac{1}{4}$" (25.4 x 18.4 cm)

16 photographs mounted back-to-back to form 11 sheets, some without images. Cover an additional 2 sheets of a thicker stock

The photographs, all of the landscape of Maine, are unidentified

Tibor de Nagy Gallery, New York. Courtesy the Estate of Rudolph Burckhardt

TRUSTEES OF THE MUSEUM OF MODERN ART